The Wadsworth Themes in American Literature Series

1800–1865

THEME 5

*The Woman Question—
and the Bachelor's Reveries*

D1611440

Shirley Samuels
Cornell University

Jay Parini
Middlebury College
General Editor

WADSWORTH
CENGAGE Learning™

Australia • Brazil • Japan • Korea • Mexico • Singapore • Spain • United Kingdom • United States

WADSWORTH
CENGAGE Learning

The Wadsworth Themes in American Literature Series, 1800–1865
Theme 5: The Woman Question—and the Bachelor's Reveries
Shirley Samuels, Jay Parini

Publisher, Humanities: *Michael Rosenberg*

Senior Development Editor: *Michell Phifer*

Assistant Editor: *Megan Garvey*

Editorial Assistant: *Rebekah Matthews*

Associate Development Project Manager: *Emily A. Ryan*

Executive Marketing Manager: *Mandee Eckersley*

Senior Marketing Communications Manager: *Stacey Purviance*

Senior Project Manager, Editorial Production: *Lianne Ames*

Senior Art Director: *Cate Rickard Barr*

Senior Print Buyer: *Mary Beth Hennebury*

Permissions Editor: *Margaret Chamberlain-Gaston*

Permissions Researcher: *Writers Research Group, LLC*

Production Service: *Kathy Smith*

Text Designer: *Frances Baca*

Photo Manager: *Sheri Blaney*

Photo Researcher: *Cheri Throop*

Cover Designer: *Frances Baca*

Cover Image: *© Hulton Archive/Getty Images*

Compositor: *Graphic World, Inc.*

For product information and technology assistance, contact us at
Cengage Learning Academic Resource Center, 1-800-423-0563
For permission to use material from this text or product, submit all requests online at **www.cengage.com/permissions.**
Further permissions questions can be e-mailed to
permissionrequest@cengage.com.

Library of Congress Control Number: 2008925313

ISBN-13: 978-1-4282-6259-1

ISBN-10: 1-4282-6259-8

Wadsworth Cengage Learning
25 Thomson Place
Boston, 02210
USA

Cengage Learning products are represented in Canada by Nelson Education, Ltd.

For your course and learning solutions, visit
academic.cengage.com.

Purchase any of our products at your local college store or at our preferred online store **www.ichapters.com.**

Printed in the United States of America
1 2 3 4 5 6 7 12 11 10 09 08

Contents

Preface

WHAT IS AMERICA? HOW HAVE WE DEFINED OURSELVES over the past five centuries, and dealt with the conflict of cultures, the clash of nations, races, ethnicities, religious visions, and class interests? How have we thought about ourselves, as men and women, in terms of class and gender? How have we managed to process a range of complex and compelling issues?

The Wadsworth Themes in American Literature Series addresses these questions in a sequence of 21 booklets designed especially for classroom use in a broad range of courses. There is nothing else like them on the market. Each booklet has been carefully edited to frame issues of importance, with attention to the development of key themes. Teachers and students have consistently found these mini-anthologies immensely productive in the classroom, as the texts we have chosen are provocative, interesting to read, and central to the era under discussion. Each thematic booklet begins with a short essay that provides the necessary historical and literary context to address the issues raised in that theme. In addition, many of the headnotes have been written by scholars, with an eye to introducing students to the life and times of the author under discussion, paying attention to historical context as well, and making sure to prepare the way for the selection that follows. The footnotes provide useful glosses on words and phrases, keying the reader to certain historical moments or ideas, explaining oddities, offering extra material to make the texts more accessible.

Each of these themes is drawn from *The Wadsworth Anthology of American Literature,* which is scheduled for later publication. The first sequence of booklets, edited by Ralph Bauer at the University of Maryland, takes in the colonial period, which runs from the arrival of Columbus in the New World through 1820, a period of immense fluidity and dynamic cultural exchange. Bauer is a pioneering scholar who takes a hemispheric approach to the era, looking at the crush of cultures—Spanish, English, Dutch, German, French; each of these European powers sent colonial missions across the Atlantic Ocean, and the collision of these cultures with each other and with the Native American population (itself diverse and complicated) was combustive. Bauer isolates several themes, one of which is called "Between Cultures," and looks at the confrontation of European and Native American traditions. In "Spirituality, Church, and State in Colonial America," he examines the obsession with religious ideas, some of which led to the crisis in Salem, where the infamous witch trials occurred. In "Empire,

Science, and the Economy in the Americas," the focus shifts to the material basis for culture, and how it affected some outlying regions, such as Barbados, Peru, Mexico, and Alaska—thus blasting apart the rigid ways that scholars have more traditionally thought about North America in isolation. In "Contested Nations in the Early Americas," Bauer centers on revolutionary fervor in places like Haiti, Cuba, and Jamaica, where various groups fought for control of both territory and cultural influence.

In the second sequence of booklets, Shirley Samuels (who chairs the English Department at Cornell and has established herself as a major voice in the field of nineteenth-century American literature) looks at the early days of the American republic, a period stretching from 1800 to 1865, taking us through the Civil War. This was, of course, a period of huge expansion as well as consolidation. Manifest Destiny was a catchword, as the original thirteen colonies expanded in what Robert Frost referred to as "a nation gradually realizing westward." The question of identity arose on different fronts, and we see the beginnings of the women's movement here. In her first theme, Samuels looks at "The Woman Question," offering a selection of texts by men and women thinking about the place of a woman in society and in the home. Some of this writing is quite provocative, and much of it is rarely studied in college classrooms.

The racial questions came into focus during this era, too, and the groundwork for the Civil War was unhappily laid. In "Confronting Race," Samuels offers a searing medley of texts from Black Hawk through Frances E. W. Harper. These works hurl this topic into stark relief against a cultural landscape in perpetual ferment. This booklet includes selections from the speeches of Sojourner Truth, the pseudonym of an astonishing black woman, a former slave who became a leading abolitionist and advocate for women's rights.

In "Manifest Destiny and the Quest for the West," Samuels offers a mix of classic and lesser known texts on the theme of westward expansion, beginning with the remarkable *Journals of Lewis and Clark*, a key document in the literature of westward expansion and a vivid example of the literature of exploration. She ends with "Views of War," presenting a range of inspiring and heart-rending texts from a time of bloodshed, hatred, and immense idealism. The Union was very nearly broken, and one gets a full sense of the dynamics of this troubled era by comparing these texts by an unusual range of authors from Oliver Wendell Holmes and Julia Ward Howe through Sidney Lanier, one of the finest (if lesser known) poets of the era.

In the third sequence of booklets, Alfred Bendixen, who teaches at Texas A&M University, offers a selection from the period just after the Civil War through the beginnings of the modern period. Bendixen, who presides over the American Literature Association, has proven himself a scholar of unusual talents, and he brings his deep knowledge of the period into play here. In "Imagining Gender," he takes up where Samuels left off, looking at a compelling range of texts by men and women who consider the evolving issue of gender in fascinating ways. One sees the coalescing of the women's movement in some of this work, and also the resistance that inevitably arose, as women tried to assert themselves and to find their voice.

In "Questions of Social and Economic Justice," Bendixen puts forward texts by a range of key figures, including George Washington Cable, Hamlin Garland, Mary Wilkins Freeman, and Jack London. Each of these gifted writers meditates on the struggle of a young nation to define itself, to locate its economic pulse, to balance the need for economic expansion and development with the requirements and demands of social justice. Many of these themes carry forward into the twentieth century, and it is worth looking closely at the origins of these themes in an era of compulsive growth. Needless to say, this was also a period when millions of immigrants arrived from Southern and Eastern Europe, radically changing the complexion of the nation. Bendixen offers a unique blend of texts on the conflicts and questions that naturally followed the so-called Great Migration in "Immigration, Ethnicity, and Race." This section includes excerpts from Jane Addams's remarkable memoir of her time at Hull-House, a mansion in Chicago where she and her coworkers offered a range of social assistance and cultural programs to working class immigrants.

The most unusual theme in this sequence of booklets by Bendixen is "Crime, Mystery, and Detection." Here the student will find an array of gripping stories by some of the original authors in a field that forms the basis for contemporary popular fiction around the world. American readers in this period loved detective stories, and readers still do. The mix is quite unusual, and it remains fascinating to see how the genre found its legs and began to run, through a time when readers wished to apply all the tools of intelligence to their world, discovering its ways and meaning, trying to figure out "who done it" in so many ways.

Martha J. Cutter—a scholar of considerable range and achievement who now teaches at the University of Connecticut—edits the sequence of booklets dealing with the modern era, 1910–1945, a period of huge importance in American history and culture. The American empire came into its own in this era, recognized its muscles, and began to flex them—in ways productive and (at times) destructive. Cutter begins by looking at the women's movement, and how men reacted to certain inevitable pressures. In "The Making of the New Woman and the New Man," she charts the struggle between the sexes in a compelling range of texts, including works by Sui Sin Far, Edwin Arlington Robinson, James Weldon Johnson, Willa Cather, and John Steinbeck, among others. Of course, the subject of class had a massive impact on how people viewed themselves, and in "Modernism and the Literary Left," she presents a selection of works that deal with issues of class, money, and power. At the center of this sequence lies "May Day," one of F. Scott Fitzgerald's most luminous and provocative stories.

The New Negro Renaissance occurred during this period, a revival and consolidation of writing in a variety of genres by African Americans. Here Cutter offers a brilliant selection of key texts from this movement, including work by Langston Hughes and Zora Neale Hurston in "Racism and Activism." This booklet extends well beyond the Harlem Renaissance itself to work by Richard Wright, a major voice in African American literature.

As it must, the theme of war occupies a central place in one thematic booklet. In the first half of the twentieth century, world wars destroyed the lives of millions. Never had the world seen killing like this, or inhumanity and cruelty on a scale that beggars the imagination. The violence of these conflicts, and the cultural implications of such destruction, necessarily held the attention of major writers. And so, in "Poetry and Fiction of War and Social Conflict," we find a range of compelling work by such writers as Ezra Pound, H.D. (Hilda Doolittle), T. S. Eliot, and Edna St. Vincent Millay.

Henry Hart is a contemporary poet, biographer, and critic with a broad range of work to his credit (he holds a chair in literature at William and Mary College). His themes are drawn from the postwar era, and he puts before readers a seductive range of work by poets, fiction writers, and essayists. Many of the themes from earlier volumes continue here. For instance, Hart begins with "Race and Ethnicity in the Melting Pot," offering students a chance to think hard about the matter of ethnicity and race in contemporary America. With texts by James Baldwin and Malcolm X through Amy Tan and Ana Menéndez, he presents viewpoints that will prove challenging and provocative—perfect vehicles for classroom discussion.

In "Class Conflicts and the American Dream," Hart explores unstable, challenging terrain in a sequence of texts by major postwar authors from Martin Luther King, Jr. through Flannery O'Connor. Some of these works are extremely well known, such as John Updike's story, "A & P." Others, such as James Merrill's "The Broken Home" may be less familiar. This booklet, as a whole, provides a rich field of texts, and will stimulate discussion on many levels about the role of class in American society.

Similarly, Hart puts forward texts that deal with gender and sexuality in "Exploring Gender and Sexual Norms." From Sylvia Plath's wildly destructive poem about her father, "Daddy," through the anguished meditations in poetry of Adrienne Rich, Anne Sexton, Allen Ginsberg, and Frank O'Hara (among others), the complexities of sexuality and relationships emerge. In Gore Vidal's witty and ferocious look at homosexuality and anti-Semitism in "Pink Triangle and Yellow Star," students have an opportunity to think hard about things that are rarely put forward in frank terms. Further meditations on masculinity and as well as gay and lesbian sexualities occur in work by Pat Califia, Robert Bly, and Mark Doty. The section called "Witnessing War" offers some remarkable poems and stories by such writers as Robert Lowell, James Dickey, and Tim O'Brien—each of them writing from a powerful personal experience. In a medley of texts on "Religion and Spirituality," Hart explores connections to the sacred, drawing on work by such writers as Flannery O'Connor, Charles Wright, and Annie Dillard. As in earlier booklets, these thematic arrangements by Hart will challenge, entertain, and instruct.

In sum, we believe these booklets will stimulate conversations in class that should be productive as well as memorable, for teacher and student alike. The texts have been chosen because of their inherent interest and readability, and—in a sense—for the multiple ways in which they "talk" to each other. Culture is, of course, nothing more than good conversation, its elevation to a level of discourse. We, the editors of these thematic booklets, believe that the attractive arrangements of compelling texts will make a lasting impression, and will help to answer the question posed at the outset: What is America?

ACKNOWLEDGMENTS

We would like to thank the following readers and scholars who helped us shape this series: Brian Adler, Valdosta State University; John Alberti, Northern Kentucky University; Lee Alexander, College of William and Mary; Althea Allard, Community College of Rhode Island; Jonathan Barron, University of Southern Mississippi; Laura Behling, Gustavus Adolphus College; Peter Bellis, University of Alabama at Birmingham; Alan Belsches, Troy University Dothan Campus; Renee Bergland, Simmons College; Roy Bird, University of Alaska Fairbanks; Michael Borgstrom, San Diego State University; Patricia Bostian, Central Peidmont Community College; Jessica Bozek, Boston University; Lenore Brady, Arizona State University; Maria Brandt, Monroe Community College; Martin Buinicki, Valparaiso University; Stuart Burrows, Brown University; Shawrence Campbell, Stetson University; Steven Canaday, Anne Arundel Community College; Carole Chapman, Ivy Tech Community College of Indiana; Cheng Lok Chua, California State University; Philip Clark, McLean High School; Matt Cohen, Duke University; Patrick Collins, Austin Community College; Paul Cook, Arizona State University; Dean Cooledge, University of Maryland Eastern Shore; Howard Cox, Angelina College; Laura Cruse, Northwest Iowa Community College; Ed Dauterich, Kent State University; Janet Dean, Bryant University; Rebecca Devers, University of Connecticut; Joseph Dewey, University of Pittsburgh–Johnstown; Christopher Diller, Berry College; Elizabeth Donely, Clark College; Stacey Donohue, Central Oregon Community College; Douglas Dowland, The University of Iowa; Jacqueline Doyle, California State University, East Bay; Robert Dunne, Central Connecticut State University; Jim Egan, Brown University; Marcus Embry, University of Northern Colorado; Nikolai Endres, Western Kentucky University; Terry Engebretsen, Idaho State University; Jean Filetti, Christopher Newport University; Gabrielle Foreman, Occidental College; Luisa Forrest, El Centro College; Elizabeth Freeman, University of California–Davis; Stephanie Freuler, Valencia Community College; Andrea Frisch, University of Maryland; Joseph Fruscione, Georgetown University; Lisa Giles, University of Southern Maine; Charles Gongre, Lamar State College–Port Arthur;

Gary Grieve-Carlson, Lebanon Valley College; Judy Harris, Tomball College; Brian Henry, University of Richmond; Allan Hikida, Seattle Central Community College; Lynn Houston, California State University, Chico; Coleman Hutchison, University of Texas–Austin; Andrew Jewell, University of Nebraska–Lincoln; Marion Kane, Lake-Sumter Community College; Laura Knight, Mercer County Community College; Delia Konzett, University of New Hampshire; Jon Little, Alverno College; Chris Lukasik, Purdue University; Martha B. Macdonald, York Technical College; Angie Macri, Pulaski Technical College; John Marsh, University of Illinois at Urbana Champaign; Christopher T. McDermot, University of Alabama; Jim McWilliams, Dickinson State University; Joe Mills, North Carolina School of the Arts; Bryan Moore, Arkansas State University; James Nagel, University of Georgia; Wade Newhouse, Peace College; Keith Newlin, University of North Carolina Wilmington; Andrew Newman, Stony Brook University; Brian Norman, Idaho State University; Scott Orme, Spokane Community College; Chris Phillips, Lafayette College; Jessica Rabin, Anne Arundel Community College; Audrey Raden, Hunter College; Catherine Rainwater, St. Edward's University; Rick Randolph, Kaua; Joan Reeves, Northeast Alabama Community College; Paul Reich, Rollins College; Yelizaveta Renfro, University of Nebraska–Lincoln; Roman Santillan, College of Staten Island; Marc Schuster, Montgomery County Community College; Carol Singley, Rutgers–Camden; Brenda Siragusa, Corinthian Colleges Inc.; John Staunton, University of North Caroline–Charlotte; Ryan Stryffeler, Ivy Tech Community College of Indiana; Robert Sturr, Kent State University, Stark Campus; James Tanner, University of North Texas; Alisa Thomas, Toccoa Falls College; Nathan Tipton, The University of Memphis; Gary Totten, North Dakota State University; Tony Trigilio, Columbia College, Chicago; Pat Tyrer, West Texas A&M University; Becky Villarreal, Austin Community College; Edward Walkiewicz, Oklahoma State University; Jay Watson, University of Mississippi; Karen Weekes, Penn State Abington; Bruce Weiner, St. Lawrence University; Cindy Weinstein, California Institute of Technology; Stephanie Wells, Orange Coast College; Robert West, Mississippi State University; Diane Whitley Bogard, Austin Community College–Eastview Campus; Edlie Wong, Rutgers; and Beth Younger, Drake University.

In addition, we would like to thank the indefatigable staff at Cengage Learning/Wadsworth for their tireless efforts to make these booklets and the upcoming anthology a reality: Michael Rosenberg, Publisher; Michell Phifer, Senior Development Editor, Lianne Ames, Senior Content Project Manager, Megan Garvey, Assistant Editor; Rebekah Matthews, Editorial Assistant, Emily Ryan, Associate Development Project Manager, Mandee Eckersley, Managing Marketing Manager, Stacey Purviance, Marketing Communications Manager, and Cate Barr, Art Director. We would also like to thank Kathy Smith, Project Manager, for her patience and attention to detail.

—Jay Parini, Middlebury College

The Woman Question— and the Bachelor's Reveries

Gender and Separate Spheres

The nineteenth century saw immense challenges to earlier formulations of identity based on race, ethnicity, gender, national origin, and class. The particular attention paid in this thematic section to how gender might be situated in a particular antebellum historical moment does not omit entirely the interconnected categories through which these selections address gender. What we now think of as women's rights initiatives were often addressed as "the woman question" before the Civil War; the questions for young men sometimes appeared, as here, in the form of an address by a "bachelor." In either case, ideas about gender often appeared in a context that has come to be called "separate spheres."

The so-called separation of spheres depended on separating the labor of men, at first agricultural and later tied to urban living, from the housekeeping and childrearing activities of women. When women joined the work force in factories, a serious challenge to this separation occurred. And when the supply of land to be distributed along the eastern seaboard began to diminish because of increasing populations, many young men began to travel to new markets and adventures, such as those supplied by the California gold rush. The words of Horace Greeley, "Go West young man!" became the rallying cry for this displacement of populations and indicated as

Unidentified artist. *Quilt* [*Album, Signature, Friendship (Massachusetts or New Hampshire)*. 1847–1862. Cotton, plain weave]
The quilt represents a communal art form practiced by women. Often such quilts would be signed by all the makers, providing artistic evidence of its collective origins.
Courtesy of the Herbert F. Johnson Museum of Art, Cornell University. Gift of Nancy Rosenthal Miller, Class of 1961, 86.060.001.

well that the population displaced was mostly male. Conversely, in the early days of textile mills, much of the laboring population was female, reflecting both the traditional association of women with sewing and the need for small fingers to work with the warp and woof of fabric.

In the early part of the nineteenth century, more than half of the population of the United States crowded along the eastern seaboard. These populations, a mixture of newly arrived immigrants in cities and earlier arrivals who had settled on farms, gathered there in part because the primary mode of transportation was by water. Early textile mills were also located along streams in order to make use of running water for energy. Rapid advances in alternative means of reaching markets and settling new communities occurred first through the development of a canal system and second through the extraordinary explosion of railroads. By the middle of the nineteenth century, much of the eastern half of what had newly become the United States was accessible through a combination of rivers, canals, and railroads. In the western regions of the United States, limited access to such means of transportation encouraged subsistence agriculture and communal organizations of people and goods. All of these economic factors, as well as heated debates about slavery, immigration, and the battles over land seizures with Mexico and other nations such as the Cherokee, affected the formative conditions for thinking about gender in terms of separate spheres.

Women's Rights

The status of women as an important issue emerged at the time of the American Revolution, was subsequently embraced by intellectuals like Mercy Otis Warren, and then became submerged under more traditional understandings of gender in the early republic. While producing compelling portraits of tormented men and women seeking adventures in the early United States, the novelist Charles Brockden Brown also concentrated on women's rights. Male supporters of women's rights did not argue that it was the "natural" right of women to be equal, but that it was socially necessary for the future health of the new nation. In arguing for such national health, Elizabeth Cady Stanton's famous "Declaration of Sentiments" of 1848 is a political document whose phrasing echoes the Declaration of Independence.

Later in the century, the renowned minister Henry Ward Beecher wrote *Woman's Influence in Politics* (1860) to support women's political involvement for the benefit of their "new spheres of influence." He argued that women in the political arena would make the United States appear more civilized. According to Beecher, giving a nod to his sisters Catharine Beecher and Harriet Beecher Stowe, civilization also meant that "women dawned into literature and changed the spirit of letters." Women becoming avid readers also changed the role of the male author: "When she became a reader, men no longer wrote as if for men." In this new world of literature, "a woman's hand is becoming more influential than the orator's mouth." Beecher

Lilly Martin Spencer, *Young Husband: First Market-ing.* [c. 1854 Hunter Museum of American Art] One of the very few successful women painters of the nineteenth century, Spencer here portrays a scene whose "reversal" of gender roles would have generated much amusement among initial view-ers. This image shows a more humorous expres-sion of general American anxiety toward "the woman question."
© *Christie's Images/CORBIS*

continued to imagine that women were separate even as he tried to dissolve differ-ences: "I do not ask, then that woman should change her nature." Keeping such a separation, and obliquely retaining gender distinctions, Beecher declared, "we want her *as* a woman, and because she is a woman—not a man." In leading to a somewhat radical political assertion, he claimed "Therefore, we seek not to unsex woman, but to unite in public affairs ... man's life and woman's life." Because of this unity, he declared, "*Woman ought to have the same right of suffrage.*" If women voted, they would refine "the broad sphere of public affairs" and "the voting of woman will be the sifting of men throughout the nation."

A milder challenge regarding gender appears in William Rounseville Alger's *The Friendships of Women* (1868). This book on friendships includes chapters on "Friendships of Women with Women," "Pairs of Female Friends," and "Needs and Duties of Women in This Age." Writing in the midst of the Civil War, when widows' losses and the dearth of men seemed to mandate other alliances, Alger presents quiet alternatives. Even as he explicitly models alternatives to romantic heterosex-ual love, he presents a discreet necessity: "There never were so many morally baf-fled, uneasy, and complaining women in the earth as now." With this "tragedy of the lonely and breaking heart," an "obscure mist of sighs exhales out of the solitude of women in the nineteenth century." The antidote, he declares, is "supplementary passions ... to assuage disappointment in one direction by securing fortifications in another." One must celebrate the friendships of women, declares the book: "No other vein of sentiment in human nature, perhaps, has so much need to be cher-ished." After defining friendship, Alger announces that it can be "the comforting substitute for love." The need for a substitute for love derives from the slaughter of so many men during the Civil War; and Alger turns bluntly to war: "war is an evil." Further, "Women, being out of it, had best keep out of it. No one desires to have women become soldiers." Such an emphasis on female friendships both confuses the matter of how women should survive the losses of war and emphasizes the relation of war to gender.

Gender and Race

What can be most difficult in describing the gender roles of the early nineteenth century in the United States is the need to account for race. In particular, there seems to be little relation between the situation of white middle-class literary women, whose sense of ambition comes into conflict with the propriety of the drawing room, and the extraordinary declarations of Sojourner Truth, whose famed rhetorical question "Aint I a woman?" is framed by the appearance of her body, her six-foot stature buttressed by the flexed muscles of her laboring arm as well as notoriously through her disclosure of the breasts that she knew her audience would associate with her gender.

Such a separation occurs as well when contrasting Frederick Douglass's account of manhood with the reveries of the conflicted bachelor who cannot decide whether single blessedness by the fireside might be preferable to the risks of loss incurred by marriage and children. Masculinity becomes a matter of class affiliation and class warfare in "The Working Men's Declaration of Independence." Indeed, the concepts of gender and labor fed inexorably into redefinitions of how home and work might exist, and contributed to debates about the use of leisure time, especially in cities.

Gender and Reform

Popular stereotypes about gender fed the stories told by writers in reform movements as they turned their attention to the enormous changes in urban and suburban populations. The tremendously popular work of the prolific novelist T. S. Arthur often involved a polemic, as in *Ten Nights in a Bar-Room, and What I Saw There*, about the appropriate vigilance of a small town in ensuring safe marriages and safe upbringing for children. In other words, the writings of men here look out for children. T. S. Arthur relates the story of the horrific decay of a small town population in part as retribution for its misguided investment in giving middle class respectability to the appalling addiction to alcohol.

The concept of reform included attention to the education of women. An important and influential early feminist, Margaret Fuller crusaded for the right of women to have access to all spheres of intellectual and political life. One of the most intelligent and most elusive women of the nineteenth century, her real genius was said to lie in conversation, and indeed she scheduled Conversations that were eagerly attended in Boston in the 1840s. Since Fuller lived in a time when "the subject of the rights and the wrongs, the joys and the griefs, the hopes and the fears, the duties and the plans, belonging to the outer and inner life of womankind in the present age, happens just now to be one of the chief matters of popular interest and agitation," her condensed expression of the significance of the relationship between men's expectations and women's performance is all the more important.

Reform questions also applied to behavior, as in the humorous comments made by Eliza Leslie on the appropriate way to handle the newly emerged category of women authors. And reform was an extremely influential aspect of journalism and urban life. Newspapers increasingly contained the work of crusading journalists, and the writings of Fanny Fern were among the most provocative and most widely read of the nineteenth century. Just as significant, the poetry of Lucy Larcom spoke for the rights of laboring women, and the poetry of Adah Isaacs Menken, sometimes defying classification, spoke a new language of women's ability to express violence and desire.

James Goodwyn Clonney, *Mother's Watch*. [Ca. 1850 Oil on canvas, 27x22 wide] Producing tranquil domestic scenes, James Goodwyn Clonney (1812–1867) reassured viewers of the harmony of rural and family life.
Courtesy Collection Westmoreland Museum of American Art, Greensburg, PA. Gift of Mr. and Mrs. Norman Hirschl, #1975.102.

Eliza Leslie 1787–1858

Eliza Leslie was born in Philadelphia in 1787 and lived in England as a child. By 1840, Leslie had become the source of conventional wisdom for all matters relating to proper etiquette and maintaining a well-run household. Her numerous works included a number of popular cookbooks, *The House Book; or, A Manual of Domestic*

Economy (1840), and *The Behaviour Book: A Manual for Ladies* (1853), a guide that advised women on the appropriate conduct in nearly any situation. Even though Leslie published fiction as well, including one novel—*Amelia; or, A Young Lady's Vicissitudes* (1848)—it was as a nineteenth-century domestic doyenne that she earned her reputation. Leslie remained an influential cultural presence until her death in 1858.

From The Behaviour Book

CHAPTER XX.

CONDUCT TO LITERARY WOMEN.

On being introduced to a female writer, it is rude to say that "you have long had a great *curiosity* to see her." Curiosity is not the right word. It is polite to imply that, "knowing her well by reputation, you are glad to have an opportunity of making her personal acquaintance." Say nothing concerning her writings, unless you chance to be alone with her. Take care not to speak of her first work as being her best; for if it is really so, she must have been retrograding from that time; a falling off that she will not like to hear of. Perhaps the truth may be, that you yourself have read only her *first* work; and if you tell her this, she will not be much flattered in supposing that you, in reality, cared so little for her first book, as to feel no desire to try a second. But she will be really gratified to learn that you are acquainted with most of her writings; and, in the course of conversation, it will be very pleasant for her to hear you quote something from them.

If she is a writer of fiction, and you presume to take the liberty of criticising her works (as you may at her own request, or if you are her intimate friend) refrain from urging that certain incidents are *improbable*, and certain characters *unnatural*. Of this it is impossible for you to judge, unless you could have lived the very same life that she has; known exactly the same people; and inhabited with her the same places. Remember always that "Truth is stranger than fiction." The French say— "Le vrai n'est pas toujours le plus vraisemblable,"—which, literally translated, means that "Truth is not always the most truthlike." Also, be it understood that a woman of quick perception and good memory can see and recollect a thousand things which would never be noticed or remembered by an obtuse or shallow, common-place capacity. And the intellect of a good writer of fiction is always brightened by the practice of taking in and laying up ideas with a view toward turning them to professional use. Trust in her, and believe that she *has* painted from life. A sensible fictionist always does. At the same time, be not too curious in questioning her as to the identity of her personages and the reality of her incidents. You have no right to expect that she will expose to you, or to any one else, her process of arranging the story, bringing out the characters, or concocting the dialogue. The machinery of her work, and the hidden springs which set it in motion, she naturally wishes to keep to

herself; and she cannot be expected to lay them bare for the gratification of impertinent curiosity, letting them become subjects of idle gossip. Be satisfied to take her
works as you find them. If you like them, read and commend them; but do not ask
her to conduct you behind the scenes, and show you the mysteries of her art—for
writing is really an art, and one that cannot be acquired, to any advantage, without
a certain amount of talent, taste, and cultivation, to say nothing of genius. What
right have you to expect that your literary friend will trust you with "the secrets of
her prison-house," and put it into your power to betray her confidence by acquaint-
ing the world that a certain popular novelist has informed you with her own lips
("but it must on no account be mentioned, as the disclosure would give mortal offence, and create for her hosts of enemies,") that by her character of Fanny Gadfly
she really means Lucy Giddings; that Mr. Hardcastle signifies Mr. Stone; that Old
Wigmore was modelled on no less a person than Isaac Baldwin; that Mrs. Baskings
was taken from Mrs. Sunning; and Mrs. Babes from Mrs. Childers—&c. &c. Also, do
not expect her to tell you on what facts her incidents were founded, and whether
there was any truth in them, or if they were mere invention.

Be not inquisitive as to the length of time consumed in writing this book or
that—or how soon the work now on hand will be finished. It can scarcely be any
concern of yours, and the writer may have reasons for keeping back the information.
Rest assured that whenever a public announcement of a new book is expedient, it
will certainly be made in print.

There are persons so rude as to question a literary woman (even on a slight acquaintance) as to the remuneration she receives for her writings—in plain terms,
"How much did you get for that? and how much are you to have for this? And how
much do you make in the course of a year? And how much a page do you get? And
how many pages can you write in a day?"

To any impertinent questions from a stranger-lady concerning the profits of
your pen, reply concisely, that these things are secrets between yourself and your
publishers. If you kindly condescend to answer without evasion, these polite enqui-
ries, you will probably hear such exclamations as, "Why, really—you must be coin-
ing money. I think I'll write books myself! There can't be a better trade," &c.

Ignorant people always suppose that popular writers are wonderfully well-
paid—and must be making rapid fortunes—because they neither starve in garrets,
nor wear rags—at least in America.

Never ask one writer what is her *real* opinion of a contemporary author. She
may be unwilling to entrust it to you, as she can have no guarantee that you will not
whisper it round till it gets into print. If she voluntarily expresses her own opinion
of another writer, and it *is* unfavourable, be honourable enough not to repeat it; but
guard it sedulously from betrayal, and avoid mentioning it to any one.

When in company with literary women, make no allusions to "learned ladies,"
or "blue stockings," or express surprise that they should have any knowledge of

housewifery, or needle-work, or dress; or that they are able to talk on "common things." It is rude and foolish, and shows that you really know nothing about them, either as a class or as individuals.

—1853

Catharine Esther Beecher 1800–1878

Catharine Beecher was an educator, author, philosopher, and reformer. The founder of schools for women and author of treatises on education and homemaking, she advocated female domesticity, expanded educational opportunities for women, and advanced the pursuit of teaching as a female profession. Her philosophy, derived from experience and study, was essentially pragmatic. Consistent with her era, she believed that women had unique traits that innately suited them to roles as wives, mothers, and educators. Although traditionalist in ascribing moral duty to sexual identity, she pioneered advances for women. She favored a full liberal arts curriculum for female students, elevated the status of homemaking to that of a domestic science, and understood the importance of providing women with adequate education and career training.

Catharine Beecher was born in East Hampton, Long Island, the eldest child of a large and prominent family. Her sister, Harriet Beecher Stowe, authored *Uncle Tom's Cabin*; her father, Lyman Beecher, was a renowned minister. The family moved to Litchfield, Connecticut, when she was ten years old. When Catharine was sixteen, her mother died and she readily assumed maternal responsibilities until her father remarried. She received a typical education for girls of her social class, but soon surpassed this modest level, teaching herself mathematics, science, Latin, and philosophy. In her twenties she taught school in New London, Connecticut. Plans for marriage were disrupted and her religious faith challenged by the sudden death of her fiancé in 1822, whereupon she resolved to remain single and "to find happiness in living to do good." In 1823, she opened a school for women, later named the Hartford Female Seminary, which expanded to over 150 students and became known for its advanced curriculum, including calisthenics and moral philosophy. She published *The Elements of Mental and Moral Philosophy, founded on Experience, Reason and the Bible* in 1831, which expressed her view that women were morally superior to men because of their capacity for self-sacrifice.

She moved westward with her father in 1832 and organized the Western Female Institute in Cincinnati, Ohio. She collaborated with William McGuffey on an elementary textbook, joined the Cincinnati temperance movement, and endorsed abolitionism to the extent that it left women in their rightful domestic sphere. Two popular books, *A Treatise on Domestic Economy* (1841) and *The Domestic Receipt Book* (1846), gave priority to the imperatives of housework and showed her technological and architectural savvy. *Treatise*, revised with Harriet Beecher Stowe, appeared as *The American Woman's Home* in 1869. Catharine Beecher traveled throughout the 1840s, lecturing and writing. In *The Duty of American Women to Their Country* (1845) she stressed the importance of training teachers, particularly to educate children in the west. She organized the American Woman's Educational Association in 1852 to accomplish her goals and also founded colleges for women in Milwaukee, Wisconsin; Dubuque, Iowa; and Quincy, Illinois. She returned to the east in the 1860s, teaching briefly at Elmira College. Resistant to the politics of late nineteenth-century feminism, she nonetheless believed that women wielded great public power through their work in homes and schools. Beecher died in Elmira, New York in 1878.

Further Reading Jeanne Boydston, Mary Kelley, and Anne Margolis, *The Limits of Sisterhood: The Beecher Sisters on Women's Rights and Woman's Sphere* (1988); Catherine Villanueva Gardner, "Heaven-Appointed Educators of Mind: Catharine Beecher and the Moral Power of Women" *Hypatia* 19.2 (2004): 1–16; Kathryn Kish Sklar, *Catharine Beecher: A Study in American Domesticity* (1973); Nicole Tonkovich, *Domesticity with a Difference: The Nonfiction of Catharine Beecher, Sarah J. Hale, Fanny Fern, and Margaret Fuller* (1997); Barbara A. White, *The Beecher Sisters* (2003).

—*Carol J. Singley, Rutgers University, Camden*

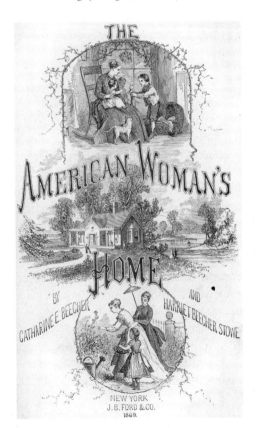

American Woman's Home; or, Principles of Domestic Science. Catharine Beecher originally published her *Principles of Domestic Science* in the 1840s to energize a sense of the importance of domesticity for American women. After her younger sister, Harriet Beecher Stowe, became a famous writer, the two collaborated on a revision that expanded the concepts of home management to discussions of how to design homes and how to concoct medications. As an innovative way of organizing the domestic space of the kitchen, Beecher's illustrations suggested that the business of running a home could be constructed in a logical and even scientific way.
Courtesy of Harriet Beecher Stowe Center, Hartford, CT

From The American Woman's Home

TO

THE WOMEN OF AMERICA,

IN WHOSE HANDS REST THE REAL DESTINIES OF THE REPUBLIC, AS
MOULDED BY THE EARLY TRAINING AND PRESERVED
AMID THE MATURER INFLUENCES OF HOME,
THIS VOLUME IS

AFFECTIONATELY INSCRIBED.

THE AMERICAN WOMAN'S HOME.

INTRODUCTION.

THE AUTHORS of this volume, while they sympathize with every honest effort to re-
lieve the disabilities and sufferings of their sex, are confident that the chief cause of
these evils is the fact that the honor and duties of the family state are not duly ap-
preciated, that women are not trained for these duties as men are trained for their
trades and professions, and that, as the consequence, family labor is poorly done,
poorly paid, and regarded as menial and disgraceful.

To be the nurse of young children, a cook, or a housemaid, is regarded as the
lowest and last resort of poverty, and one which no woman of culture and position
can assume without loss of caste and respectability.

It is the aim of this volume to elevate both the honor and the remuneration of
all the employments that sustain the many difficult and sacred duties of the family
state, and thus to render each department of woman's true profession as much de-
sired and respected as are the most honored professions of men.

When the other sex are to be instructed in law, medicine, or divinity, they are
favored with numerous institutions richly endowed, with teachers of the highest
talents and acquirements, with extensive libraries, and abundant and costly appara-
tus. With such advantages they devote nearly ten of the best years of life to preparing
themselves for their profession; and to secure the public from unqualified members
of these professions, none can enter them until examined by a competent body, who
certify to their due preparation for their duties.

Woman's profession embraces the care and nursing of the body in the critical
periods of infancy and sickness, the training of the human mind in the most im-
pressible period of childhood, the instruction and control of servants, and most
of the government and economies of the family state. These duties of woman
are as sacred and important as any ordained to man; and yet no such advantages
for preparation have been accorded to her, nor is there any qualified body to certify the public that a woman is duly prepared to give proper instruction in her
profession.

This unfortunate want, and also the questions frequently asked concerning the domestic qualifications of both the authors of this work, who have formerly written upon such topics, make it needful to give some account of the advantage they have enjoyed in preparation for the important office assumed as teachers of woman's domestic duties.

XV

DOMESTIC MANNERS.

Good manners are the expressions of benevolence in personal intercourse, by which we endeavor to promote the comfort and enjoyment of others, and to avoid all that gives needless uneasiness. It is the exterior exhibition of the divine precept, which requires us to do to others as we would that they should do to us. It is saying, by our deportment, to all around, that we consider their feelings, tastes, and conveniences, as equal in value to our own.

Good manners lead us to avoid all practices which offend the taste of others; all unnecessary violations of the conventional rules of propriety; all rude and disrespectful language and deportment; and all remarks which would tend to wound the feelings of others.

There is a serious defect in the manners of the American people, especially among the descendants of the Puritan settlers of New-England, which can never be efficiently remedied, except in the domestic circle, and during early life. It is a deficiency in the free expression of kindly feelings and sympathetic emotions, and a want of courtesy in deportment. The causes which have led to this result may easily be traced.

The forefathers of this nation, to a wide extent, were men who were driven from their native land by laws and customs which they believed to be opposed both to civil and religious freedom. The sufferings they were called to endure, the subduing of those gentler feelings which bind us to country, kindred, and home; and the constant subordination of the passions to stern principle, induced characters of great firmness and self-control. They gave up the comforts and refinements of a civilized country, and came as pilgrims to a hard soil, a cold clime, and a heathen shore. They were continually forced to encounter danger, privations, sickness, loneliness, and death; and all these their religion taught them to meet with calmness, fortitude, and submission. And thus it became the custom and habit of the whole mass, to repress rather than to encourage the expression of feeling.

Persons who are called to constant and protracted suffering and privation are forced to subdue and conceal emotion; for the free expression of it would double their own suffering, and increase the sufferings of others. Those, only, who are free from care and anxiety, and whose minds are mainly occupied by cheerful emotions, are at full liberty to unvail their feelings.

It was under such stern and rigorous discipline that the first children in New-England were reared; and the manners and habits of parents are usually, to a great extent, transmitted to children. Thus it comes to pass, that the descendants of the Puritans, now scattered over every part of the nation, are predisposed to conceal the gentler emotions, while their manners are calm, decided, and cold, rather than free and impulsive. Of course, there are very many exceptions to these predominating characteristics.

Other causes to which we may attribute a general want of courtesy in manners are certain incidental results of our domestic institutions. Our ancestors and their descendants have constantly been combating the aristocratic principle which would exalt one class of men at the expense of another. They have had to contend with this principle, not only in civil but in social life. Almost every American, in his own person as well as in behalf of his class, has had to assume and defend the main principle of democracy—that every man's feelings and interests are equal in value to those of every other man. But, in doing this, there has been some want of clear discrimination. Because claims based on distinctions of mere birth, fortune, or position, were found to be injurious, many have gone to the extreme of inferring that all distinctions, involving subordinations, are useless. Such would wrongfully regard children as equals to parents, pupils to teachers, domestics to their employers, and subjects to magistrates—and that, too, in all respects.

The fact that certain grades of superiority and subordination are needful, both for individual and public benefit, has not been clearly discerned; and there has been a gradual tendency to an extreme of the opposite view which has sensibly affected our manners. All the proprieties and courtesies which depend on the recognition of the relative duties of superior and subordinate have been warred upon; and thus we see, to an increasing extent, disrespectful treatment of parents, by children; of teachers, by pupils; of employers, by domestics; and of the aged, by the young. In all classes and circles, there is a gradual decay in courtesy of address.

In cases, too, where kindness is rendered, it is often accompanied with a cold, unsympathizing manner, which greatly lessens its value; while kindness or politeness is received in a similar style of coolness, as if it were but the payment of a just due.

It is owing to these causes that the American people, especially the descendants of the Puritans, do not do themselves justice. For, while those who are near enough to learn their real character and feelings can discern the most generous impulses, and the most kindly sympathies, they are often so vailed behind a composed and indifferent demeanor, as to be almost entirely concealed from strangers.

These defects in our national manners it especially falls to the care of mothers, and all who have charge of the young, to rectify; and if they seriously undertake the matter, and wisely adapt means to ends, these defects will be remedied. With reference to this object, the following ideas are suggested.

The law of Christianity and of democracy, which teaches that all men are born equal in rights, and that their interests and feelings should be regarded as of equal value, seems to be adopted in aristocratic circles, with exclusive reference to the class in which the individual moves. The courtly gentleman addresses all of his own class with politeness and respect; and in all his actions, seems to allow that the feelings and convenience of these others are to be regarded the same as his own. But his demeanor to those of inferior station is not based on the same rule.

Among those who make up aristocratic circles, such as are above them are deemed of superior, and such as are below of inferior, value. Thus, if a young, ignorant, and vicious coxcomb happens to have been born a lord, the aged, the virtuous, the learned, and the well-bred of another class must give his convenience the precedence, and must address him in terms of respect. So sometimes, when a man of "noble birth" is thrown among the lower classes, he demeans himself in a style which, to persons of his own class, would be deemed the height of assumption and rudeness.

Now, the principles of democracy require that the same courtesy which we accord to our own circle shall be extended to every class and condition; and that distinctions of superiority and subordination shall depend, not on accidents of birth, fortune, or occupation, but solely on those mutual relations which the good of all classes equally require. The distinctions demanded in a democratic state are simply those which result from relations that are common to every class, and are for the benefit of all.

It is for the benefit of every class that children be subordinate to parents, pupils to teachers, the employed to their employers, and subjects to magistrates. In addition to this, it is for the general well-being that the comfort or convenience of the delicate and feeble should be preferred to that of the strong and healthy, who would suffer less by any deprivation; that precedence should be given to their elders by the young; and that reverence should be given to the hoary head.

The rules of good-breeding, in a democratic state, must be founded on these principles. It is indeed assumed that the value of the happiness of each individual is the same as that of every other; but as there must be occasions where there are advantages which all can not enjoy, there must be general rules for regulating a selection. Otherwise, there would be constant scrambling among those of equal claims, and brute force must be the final resort; in which case, the strongest would have the best of every thing. The democratic rule, then, is, that superiors in age, station, or office have precedence of subordinates; age and feebleness, of youth and strength; and the feebler sex, of more vigorous man.*

---

* The universal practice of this nation, in thus giving precedence to woman has been severely commented on by foreigners, and by some who would transfer all the business of the other sex to women, and then have them treated like men. But we hope this evidence of our superior civilization and Christianity may increase rather than diminish.

There is, also, a style of deportment and address which is appropriate to these different relations. It is suitable for a superior to secure compliance with his wishes from those subordinate to him by commands; but a subordinate must secure compliance with his wishes from a superior by requests. (Although the kind and considerate manner to subordinates will always be found the most effective as well as the pleasantest, by those in superior station.) It is suitable for a parent, teacher, or employer to admonish for neglect of duty; but not for an inferior to adopt such a course toward a superior. It is suitable for a superior to take precedence of a subordinate, without any remark; but not for an inferior, without previously asking leave, or offering an apology. It is proper for a superior to use language and manners of freedom and familiarity, which would be improper from a subordinate to a superior.

The want of due regard to these proprieties occasions a great defect in American manners. It is very common to hear children talk to their parents in a style proper only between companions and equals; so, also, the young address their elders; those employed, their employers; and domestics, the members of the family and their visitors, in a style which is inappropriate to their relative positions. But courteous address is required not merely toward superiors; every person desires to be thus treated, and therefore the law of benevolence demands such demeanor toward all whom we meet in the social intercourse of life. "Be ye courteous," is the direction of the apostle in reference to our treatment of *all*.

Good manners can be successfully cultivated only in early life and in the domestic circle. There is nothing which depends so much upon *habit* as the constantly recurring proprieties of good breeding; and if a child grows up without forming such habits, it is very rarely the case that they can be formed at a later period. The feeling that it is of little consequence how we behave at home if we conduct ourselves properly abroad, is a very fallacious one. Persons who are careless and ill-bred at home may imagine that they can assume good manners abroad; but they mistake. Fixed habits of tone, manner, language, and movements can not be suddenly altered; and those who are ill-bred at home, even when they try to hide their bad habits, are sure to violate many of the obvious rules of propriety, and yet be unconscious of it.

And there is nothing which would so effectually remove prejudice against our democratic institutions as the general cultivation of good-breeding in the domestic circle. Good manners are the exterior of benevolence, the minute and constant exhibitions of "peace and good-will;" and the nation, as well as the individual, which most excels in the external demonstration, as well as the internal principle, will be most respected and beloved.

It is only the training of the family state according to its true end and aim that is to secure to woman her true position and rights. When the family is instituted by marriage, it is man who is the head and chief magistrate by the force of his physical power and requirement of the chief responsibility; not less is he so according to the

Christian law, by which, when differences arise, the husband has the deciding control, and the wife is to obey. "Where love is, there is no law;" but where love is not, the only dignified and peaceful course is for the wife, however much his superior, to "submit, as to God and not to man."

But this power of nature and of religion, given to man as the controlling head, involves the distinctive duty of the family state, *self-sacrificing love*. The husband is to "honor" the wife, to love her as himself, and thus account her wishes and happiness as of equal value with his own. But more than this, he is to love her "as Christ loved the Church;" that is, he is to "suffer" for her, if need be, in order to support and elevate and ennoble her.

The father then is to set the example of self-sacrificing love and devotion; and the mother, of Christian obedience when it is required. Every boy is to be trained for his future domestic position by labor and sacrifices for his mother and sisters. It is the brother who is to do the hardest and most disagreeable work, to face the storms and perform the most laborious drudgeries. In the family circle, too, he is to give his mother and sister precedence in all the conveniences and comforts of home life.

It is only those nations where the teachings and example of Christ have had most influence that man has ever assumed his obligations of self-sacrificing benevolence in the family. And even in Christian communities, the duty of wives to obey their husbands has been more strenuously urged than the obligations of the husband to love his wife "as Christ loved the Church."

Here it is needful to notice that the distinctive duty of obedience to man does not rest on women who do not enter the relations of married life. A woman who inherits property, or who earns her own livelihood, can institute the family state, adopt orphan children and employ suitable helpers in training them; and then to her will appertain the authority and rights that belong to man as the head of a family. And when every woman is trained to some self-supporting business, she will not be tempted to enter the family state as a subordinate, except by that love for which there is no need of law.

These general principles being stated, some details in regard to domestic manners will be enumerated.

In the first place, there should be required in the family a strict attention to the rules of precedence, and those modes of address appropriate to the various relations to be sustained. Children should always be required to offer their superiors, in age or station, the precedence in all comforts and conveniences, and always address them in a respectful tone and manner. The custom of adding, "Sir," or "Ma'am," to "Yes," or "No," is valuable, as a perpetual indication of a respectful recognition of superiority. It is now going out of fashion, even among the most well bred people; probably from a want of consideration of its importance. Every remnant of courtesy of address, in our customs, should be carefully cherished, by all who feel a value for the proprieties of good breeding.

If parents allow their children to talk to them, and to the grown persons in the family, in the same style in which they address each other, it will be in vain to hope for the courtesy of manner and tone which good breeding demands in the general intercourse of society. In a large family, where the elder children are grown up, and the younger are small, it is important to require the latter to treat the elder in some sense as superiors. There are none so ready as young children to assume airs of equality; and if they are allowed to treat one class of superiors in age and character disrespectfully, they will soon use the privilege universally. This is the reason why the youngest children of a family are most apt to be pert, forward, and unmannerly.

Another point to be aimed at is, to require children always to acknowledge every act of kindness and attention, either by words or manner. If they are so trained as always to make grateful acknowledgments, when receiving favors, one of the objectionable features in American manners will be avoided.

Again, children should be required to ask leave, whenever they wish to gratify curiosity, or use an article which belongs to another. And if cases occur, when they can not comply with the rules of good-breeding, as, for instance, when they must step between a person and the fire, or take the chair of an older person, they should be taught either to ask leave, or to offer an apology.

There is another point of good-breeding, which can not, in all cases, be understood and applied by children in its widest extent. It is that which requires us to avoid all remarks which tend to embarrass, vex, mortify, or in any way wound the feelings of another. To notice personal defects; to allude to others' faults, or the faults of their friends; to speak disparagingly of the sect or party to which a person belongs; to be inattentive when addressed in conversation; to contradict flatly; to speak in contemptuous tones of opinions expressed by another; all these are violations of the rules of good-breeding, which children should be taught to regard. Under this head comes the practice of whispering and staring about, when a teacher, or lecturer, or clergyman is addressing a class or audience. Such inattention is practically saying that what the person is uttering is not worth attending to; and persons of real good-breeding always avoid it. Loud talking and laughing in a large assembly, even when no exercises are going on; yawning and gaping in company; and not looking in the face a person who is addressing you, are deemed marks of ill-breeding.

Another branch of good manners relates to the duties of hospitality. Politeness requires us to welcome visitors with cordiality; to offer them the best accommodations; to address conversation to them; and to express, by tone and manner, kindness and respect. Offering the hand to all visitors at one's own house is a courteous and hospitable custom; and a cordial shake of the hand, when friends meet, would abate much of the coldness of manner ascribed to Americans.

Another point of good breeding refers to the conventional rules of propriety and good taste. Of these, the first class relates to the avoidance of all disgusting or offensive personal habits: such as fingering the hair; obtrusively using a toothpick, or carrying one in the mouth after the needful use of it; cleaning the nails in presence of others; picking the nose; spitting on carpets; snuffing instead of using a handkerchief, or using the article in an offensive manner; lifting up the boots or shoes, as some men do, to tend them on the knee, or to finger them: all these tricks, either at home or in society, children should be taught to avoid.

Another topic, under this head, may be called *table manners*. To persons of good-breeding, nothing is more annoying than violations of the conventional proprieties of the table. Reaching over another person's plate; standing up, to reach distant articles, instead of asking to have them passed; using one's own knife and spoon for butter, salt, or sugar, when it is the custom of the family to provide separate utensils for the purpose; setting cups with the tea dripping from them, on the table-cloth, instead of the mats or small plates furnished; using the table-cloth instead of the napkins; eating fast, and in a noisy manner; putting large pieces in the mouth; looking and eating as if very hungry, or as if anxious to get at certain dishes; sitting at too great a distance from the table, and dropping food; laying the knife and fork on the table-cloth, instead of on the edge of the plate; picking the teeth at table: all these particulars children should be taught to avoid.

It is always desirable, too, to train children, when at table with grown persons, to be silent, except when addressed by others; or else their chattering will interrupt the conversation and comfort of their elders. They should always be required, too, to wait in silence, till all the older persons are helped.

When children are alone with their parents, it is desirable to lead them to converse and to take this as an opportunity to form proper conversational habits. But it should be a fixed rule that, when strangers are present, the children are to listen in silence and only reply when addressed. Unless this is secured, visitors will often be condemned to listen to puerile chattering, with small chance of the proper attention due to guests and superiors in age and station.

Children should be trained, in preparing themselves for the table or for appearance among the family, not only to put their hair, face, and hands in neat order, but also their nails, and to habitually attend to this latter whenever they wash their hands.

There are some very disagreeable tricks which many children practice even in families counted well-bred. Such, for example, are drumming with the fingers on some piece of furniture, or humming a tune while others are talking, or interrupting conversation by pertinacious questions, or whistling in the house instead of outdoors, or speaking several at once and in loud voices to gain attention. All these are violations of good-breeding, which children should be trained to avoid, lest they should not only annoy as children, but practice the same kind of ill manners when mature. In all assemblies for public debate, a chairman or moderator is appointed whose business it is to see that only one person speaks at a time, that no one interrupts a person when speaking, that no needless noises are made, and that all indecorums are avoided. Such an officer is sometimes greatly needed in family circles.

Children should be encouraged freely to use lungs and limbs out-doors, or in hours for sport in the house. But at other times, in the domestic circle, gentle tones and manners should be cultivated. The words *gentleman* and *gentlewoman* came originally from the fact that the uncultivated and ignorant classes used coarse and loud tones, and rough words and movements; while only the refined circles habitually used gentle tones and gentle manners. For the same reason, those born in the higher circles were called "of gentle blood." Thus it came that a coarse and loud voice, and rough, ungentle manners, are regarded as vulgar and plebeian.

All these things should be taught to children, gradually, and with great patience and gentleness. Some parents, with whom good manners are a great object, are in danger of making their children perpetually uncomfortable, by suddenly surrounding them with so many rules that they must inevitably violate some one or other a great part of the time. It is much better to begin with a few rules, and be steady and persevering with these, till a habit is formed, and then take a few more, thus making the process easy and gradual. Otherwise, the temper of children will be injured; or, hopeless of fulfilling so many requisitions, they will become reckless and indifferent to all.

If a few brief, well-considered, and sensible rules of good manners could be suspended in every school-room, and the children all required to commit them to memory, it probably would do more to remedy the defects of American manners and to advance universal good-breeding than any other mode that could be so easily adopted.

But, in reference to those who have enjoyed advantages for the cultivation of good manners, and who duly estimate its importance, one caution is necessary. Those who never have had such habits formed in youth are under disadvantages which no benevolence of temper can altogether remedy. They may often violate the tastes and feelings of others, not from a want of proper regard for them, but from ignorance of custom, or want of habit, or abstraction of mind, or from other causes which demand forbearance and sympathy, rather than displeasure. An ability to bear patiently with defects in manners, and to make candid and considerate allowance for a want of advantages, or for peculiarities in mental habits, is one mark of the benevolence of real good-breeding.

The advocates of monarchical and aristocratic institutions have always had great plausibility given to their views, by the seeming tendencies of our institutions to insubordination and bad manners. And it has been too indiscriminately conceded, by the defenders of the latter, that such are these tendencies, and that the offensive points in American manners are the necessary result of democratic principles.

But it is believed that both facts and reasoning are in opposition to this opinion. The following extract from the work of De Tocqueville, the great political philosopher of France, exhibits the opinion of an impartial observer, when comparing American manners with those of the English, who are confessedly the most aristocratic of all people.

He previously remarks on the tendency of aristocracy to make men more sympathizing with persons of their own peculiar class, and less so toward those of lower degree; and he then contrasts American manners with the English, claiming that the Americans are much the more affable, mild, and social. "In America, where the privileges of birth never existed and where riches confer no peculiar rights on their possessors, men acquainted with each other are very ready to frequent the same places, and find neither peril nor disadvantage in the free interchange of their thoughts. If they meet by accident, they neither seek nor avoid intercourse; their manner is therefore natural, frank, and open." "If their demeanor is often cold and serious, it is never haughty or constrained." But an "aristocratic pride is still extremely great among the English; and as the limits of aristocracy are still ill-defined, every body lives in constant dread, lest advantage should be taken of his familiarity. Unable to judge, at once, of the social position of those he meets, an Englishman prudently avoids all contact with him. Men are afraid, lest some slight service rendered should draw them into an unsuitable acquaintance; they dread civilities, and they avoid the obtrusive gratitude of a stranger, as much as his hatred."

Thus, *facts* seem to show that when the most aristocratic nation in the world is compared, as to manners, with the most democratic, the judgment of strangers is in favor of the latter. And if good manners are the outward exhibition of the democratic principle of impartial benevolence and equal rights, surely the nation which adopts this rule, both in social and civil life, is the most likely to secure the desirable exterior. The aristocrat, by his principles, extends the exterior of impartial benevolence to his own class only; the democratic principle requires it to be extended *to all*.

There is reason, therefore, to hope and expect more refined and polished manners in America than in any other land; while all the developments of taste and refinement, such as poetry, music, painting, sculpture, and architecture, it may be expected, will come to as high a state of perfection here as in any other nation.

If this country increases in virtue and intelligence, as it may, there is no end to the wealth which will pour in as the result of our resources of climate, soil, and navigation, and the skill, industry, energy, and enterprise of our countrymen. This wealth, if used as intelligence and virtue dictate, will furnish the means for a superior education to all classes, and every facility for the refinement of taste, intellect, and feeling.

Moreover, in this country, labor is ceasing to be the badge of a lower class; so that already it is disreputable for a man to be "a lazy gentleman." And this feeling must increase, till there is such an equalization of labor as will afford all the time needful for every class to improve the many advantages offered to them. Already through the munificence of some of our citizens, there are literary and scientific advantages offered to all classes, rarely enjoyed elsewhere. In most of our large cities and towns, the advantages of education, now offered to the poorest classes, often without charge, surpass what, some years ago, most wealthy men could purchase for any price. And it is believed that a time will come when the poorest boy in America can secure advantages, which will equal what the heir of the proudest peerage can now command.

The records of the courts of France and Germany, (as detailed by the Duchess of Orleans,) in and succeeding the brilliant reign of Louis the Fourteenth—a period which was deemed the acme of elegance and refinement—exhibit a grossness, a vulgarity, and a coarseness, not to be found among the very lowest of our respectable poor. And the biography of the English Beau Nash, who attempted to reform the manners of the gentry, in the times of Queen Anne, exhibits violations of the rules of decency among the aristocracy, which the commonest yeoman of this land would feel disgraced in perpetrating.

This shows that our lowest classes, at this period, are more refined than were the highest in aristocratic lands, a hundred years ago; and another century may show the lowest classes, in wealth, in this country, attaining as high a polish as adorns those who now are leaders of good manners in the courts of kings.

—1869

George Henry Evans 1805–1856

George Henry Evans was born in England in 1805 and moved to upstate New York with his family in 1820. Evans became a printer and publisher after an early apprenticeship and soon had his own printing company. In 1829, Evans began editing and publishing the *Working Man's Advocate*, the second labor newspaper to be published in the United States. The paper broadly addressed labor reform, and the publication of "The Working Men's Declaration of Independence" highlighted the key grievances of the movement, including issues of taxation and laws that were unfair to workers. By 1841, Evans had become increasingly concerned with the issue of public lands in the West, which he felt should be given to settlers. In support of this view, he founded the National Reform Association in 1844. Evans is credited as a central figure in the passage of the 1862 Homestead Act, which would eventually make the land distribution goals of the Association a reality.

The Working Men's Declaration of Independence

"When in the course of human events, it becomes necessary" for one class of a community to assert their natural and unalienable rights in opposition to other classes of their fellow men, "and to assume among" them a political "station of equality to which the laws of nature and of nature's God," as well as the principles of their political compact, "entitle them; a decent respect to the opinions of mankind," and the more paramount duty they owe to their own fellow citizens, "requires that they should declare the causes which impel them" to adopt so painful, yet so necessary, a measure.

"We hold these truths to be self evident, that all men are *created equal;* that they are endowed by their creator with certain unalienable rights; that among these are *life, liberty,* and the *pursuit of happiness;* that to secure these rights" against the undue influence of other classes of society, prudence, as well as the claims of self defence, dictates the necessity of the organization of a party, who shall, by their representatives, prevent dangerous combinations to subvert these indefeasible and fundamental privileges. "All experience hath shown, that mankind" in general, and *we as a class in particular,* "are more disposed to suffer, while evils are sufferable, than to right themselves," by an opposition which the pride and self interest of unprincipled political aspirants, with the more unprincipled zeal of religious bigotry, will wilfully misrepresent. "But when a long train of abuses and usurpations" take place, all invariably tending to the oppression and degradation of one class of society, and to the unnatural and iniquitous exaltation of another by political leaders, "it is their right, it is their duty," to use every constitutional means to *reform* the abuses of such a government, and to provide new guards for their future security. The history of the political *parties* in this state, is a history of political *iniquities,* all tending to the enacting and enforcing oppressive and unequal laws. To prove this, let facts be submitted to the candid and impartial of our fellow citizens of all parties.

1. The laws for levying taxes are all based on erroneous principles, in consequence of their operating most oppressively on one class of society, and being scarcely felt by the other.

2. The laws regarding the duties of jurors, witnesses, and militia trainings, are still more unequal and oppressive.

3. The laws for private incorporations are all partial in their operations forming one class of society to the expense of the other, who have no equal participation.

4. The laws incorporating religious societies have a pernicious tendency, by promoting the erection of magnificent places of public worship, by the rich, excluding others, and which others cannot imitate; consequently engendering spiritual pride in the clergy and people, and thereby creating odious distinctions in society, destructive to its social peace and happiness.

5. The laws establishing and patronizing seminaries of learning are unequal, favoring the rich, and perpetuating imparity, which natural causes have produced, and which judicious laws ought, and can, remedy.

6. The laws and municipal ordinances and regulations, generally, besides those specially enumerated, have heretofore been ordained on such principles, as have deprived nine tenths of the members of the body politic, who are *not* wealthy, of the *equal means* to enjoy *"life, liberty, and the pursuit of happiness,"* which the *rich* enjoy exclusively; but which the federative compact intended to secure to all, indiscriminately. The lien law in favor of landlords against tenants, and all other honest creditors, is one illustration among innumerable others which can be adduced to prove the truth of these allegations.

We have trusted to the influence of the justice and good sense of our political leaders, to prevent the continuance of these abuses, which destroy the natural bands of equality, so essential to the attainment of moral happiness; "but they have been deaf alike to the voice of justice and of consanguinity."

Therefore, we, the working class of society, of the city of New York, "appealing to the supreme judge of the world," and to the reason and consciences of the impartial of all parties, "for the rectitude of our intentions, do, in the spirit, and by the authority," of that political liberty which has been promised to us equally with our fellow men, solemnly publish and declare, and invite all under like pecuniary circumstances, together with every liberal mind, to join us in the declaration, "that we are, and of right ought to be," entitled to EQUAL MEANS to obtain equal moral happiness, and social enjoyment, and that all lawful and constitutional measures ought to be adopted to the attainment of those objects. "And for the support of this declaration, we mutually pledge to each other" our faithful aid to the end of our lives.

This declaration of our rights, and brief allegation of our grievances, will, I am confident be welcomed by more than three fourths of the members of this nation. There wants but a determined moral courage to support them against designing and interested partizans, in order to secure those great blessings for ourselves and for posterity.

The seeds of moral happiness are sown with as unbounded a liberality, as are those so necessary for our physical wants. To the attainment of even the latter, in any degree of perfection, labor and toil, with great intellectual exertions, are, by the invariable laws of nature, indispensable. Even so with our moral happiness; it is only through the discreet and judicious exercise of our mental powers that we can attain any degree of felicity. The bane of every nation on the face of the earth, has been the debased state of PUBLIC OPINION; a wicked and an unprincipled *few* have given tone to it, and the honest *many* have submitted to their own consequent degradation. A moral *influence*, fatal to our social enjoyment, has usurped the power, where the full exertion of our intellectual faculties ought to control and to govern us. The crisis has now arrived. To obtain our political and religious rights, *collectively*, we must exert our moral courage *individually*. The voice of nature loudly calls for these exertions, and the sacred claims of families and posterity repeats the call in mental echoes.

—1829

T. S. Arthur 1809–1885

A journalist, children's book author, novelist, and editor, Timothy Shay Arthur is best known for his 1854 novel, *Ten Nights in a Bar-Room, and What I Saw There.* An immensely popular and prolific writer, Arthur is often credited with producing over 5 percent of all American fiction published during the decade of the 1840s. T. S. Arthur was born in 1809 in Orange County, New York and married Eliza Alden in 1836. The couple had seven children and Arthur was by all accounts an intensely devoted father who paid careful concern to their moral upbringing. When *Ten Nights in a Bar-Room* was published in 1854, it sold enormously well, thanks in part to the popularity of the temperance movement and the promotion of the novel by teetotalers. The book spawned an influential dramatization by William Pratt in 1858. *Ten Nights* traced the slow, but sure destruction of the fictional Cedarville community due to the opening of a tavern that corrupted the morals of its inhabitants and destroyed lives and families. Told through the viewpoint of Mr. Romaine—a moralizing traveler who stops and stays at Simon Slade's Sickle and Sheaf tavern for ten nights spread out over ten years—the work appeals to conventions of sentimental melodrama in its characterizations and action. Scenes like that of the death of young Mary Morgan—an innocent victim of intemperance—fueled a nation's fascination with social reform and martyrdom. Despite his failing health and a gradual loss of eyesight, Arthur remained active in social and religious causes and performed various editorial duties nearly until his death in 1885.

From Ten Nights in a Bar-Room

NIGHT THE FIRST.

The "Sickle and Sheaf.:"

Ten years ago, business required me to pass a day in Cedarville. It was late in the afternoon when the stage set me down at the "Sickle and Sheaf," a new tavern, just opened by a new landlord, in a new house, built with the special end of providing "accommodations for man and beast." As I stepped from the dusty old vehicle in which I had been jolted along a rough road for some thirty miles, feeling tired and hungry, the good-natured face of Simon Slade, the landlord, beaming as it did with a hearty welcome, was really a pleasant sight to see, and the grasp of his hand was like that of a true friend.

I felt, as I entered the new and neatly furnished sitting-room adjoining the bar, that I had indeed found a comfortable resting-place after my wearisome journey.

"All as nice as a new pin," said I, approvingly, as I glanced around the room, up to the ceiling—white as the driven snow—and over the handsomely carpeted floor. "Haven't seen any thing so inviting as this. How long have you been open?"

"Only a few months," answered the gratified landlord. "But we are not yet in good going order. It takes time, you know, to bring every thing into the right shape. Have you dined yet?"

"No. Every thing looked so dirty at the stage-house where we stopped to get dinner, that I couldn't venture upon the experiment of eating. How long before your supper will be ready?"

"In an hour," replied the landlord.

"That will do. Let me have a nice piece of tender steak, and the loss of dinner will soon be forgotten."

"You shall have that, cooked fit for an alderman," said the landlord. "I call my wife the best cook in Cedarville."

As he spoke, a neatly dressed girl, about sixteen years of age, with rather an attractive countenance, passed through the room.

"My daughter," said the landlord, as she vanished through the door. There was a sparkle of pride in the father's eyes, and a certain tenderness in the tones of his voice, as he said—"My daughter," that told me she was very dear to him.

"You are a happy man to have so fair a child," said I, speaking more in compliment than with a careful choice of words.

"I am a happy man," was the landlord's smiling answer; his fair, round face, unwrinkled by a line of care or trouble, beaming with self-satisfaction. "I have always been a happy man, and always expect to be. Simon Slade takes the world as it comes, and takes it easy. My son, sir"—he added, as a boy in his twelfth year, came in. "Speak to the gentleman."

The boy lifted to mine a pair of deep blue eyes, from which innocence beamed, as he offered me his hand, and said, respectfully—"How do you do, sir?" I could not but remark the girl-like beauty of his face, in which the hardier firmness of the boy's character was already visible.

"What is your name?" I asked.

"Frank, sir."

"Frank is his name," said the landlord—"we called him after his uncle. Frank and Flora—the names sound pleasant to our ears. But, you know, parents are apt to be a little partial and over fond."

"Better that extreme than its opposite," I remarked.

"Just what I always say. Frank, my son"—the landlord spoke to the boy, "there's some one in the bar. You can wait on him as well as I can."

The lad glided from the room, in ready obedience.

"A handy boy that, sir; a very handy boy. Almost as good in the bar as a man. He mixes a toddy or a punch just as well as I can."

"But," I suggested, "are you not a little afraid of placing one so young in the way of temptation."

"Temptation!" The open brows of Simon Slade contracted a little. "No, sir!" he replied, emphatically. "The till is safer under his care than it would be in that of one man in ten. The boy comes, sir, of honest parents. Simon Slade never wronged anybody out of a farthing."

"Oh," said I, quickly, "you altogether misapprehend me. I had no reference to the till, but to the bottle."

The landlord's brows were instantly unbent, and a broad smile circled over his good-humoured face.

"Is that all? Nothing to fear, I can assure you. Frank has no taste for liquor, and might pour it out for months without a drop finding its way to his lips. Nothing to apprehend there, sir—nothing."

I saw that further suggestions of danger would be useless, and so remained silent. The arrival of a traveller called away the landlord, and I was left alone for observation and reflection. The bar adjoined the neat sitting-room, and I could see, through the open door, the customer upon whom the lad was attending. He was a well-dressed young man—or rather boy, for he did not appear to be over nineteen years of age—with a fine, intelligent face, that was already slightly marred by sensual indulgence. He raised the glass to his lips, with a quick, almost eager motion, and drained it at a single draught.

"Just right," said he, tossing a sixpence to the young bar-tender. "You are first-rate at a brandy-toddy. Never drank a better in my life."

The lad's smiling face told that he was gratified by the compliment. To me the sight was painful, for I saw that this youthful tippler was on dangerous ground.

"Who is that young man in the bar?" I asked, a few minutes afterward, on being rejoined by the landlord.

Simon Slade stepped to the door and looked into the bar for a moment. Two or three men were there by this time; but he was at no loss in answering my question.

"Oh, that's a son of Judge Hammond, who lives in the large brick house just as you enter the village. Willy Hammond, as everybody familiarly calls him, is about the finest young man in our neighbourhood. There is nothing proud or put-on about him—nothing—even if his father is a judge, and rich into the bargain. Every one, gentle or simple, likes Willy Hammond. And then he is such good company. Always so cheerful, and always with a pleasant story on his tongue. And he's so high-spirited withal, and so honourable. Willy Hammond would lose his right hand rather than be guilty of a mean action."

* * *

Ten o'clock found me alone and musing in the bar room over the occurrences of the evening. Of all the incidents, that of the entrance of Joe Morgan's child kept the most prominent place in my thoughts. The picture of that mournful little face was ever before me; and I seemed all the while to hear the word "Father," uttered so touchingly, and yet with such a world of childish tenderness. And the man, who would have opposed the most stubborn resistance to his fellow men, had they sought to force him from the room, going passively, almost meekly out, led by that little child—I could not, for a time, turn my thoughts from the image thereof! And then thought bore me to the wretched home, back to which the gentle, loving child had taken her father, and my heart grew faint in me as imagination busied itself with all the misery there.

And Willy Hammond. The little that I had heard and seen of him greatly interested me in his favour Ah! upon what dangerous ground was he treading. How many pitfalls awaited his feet—how near they were to the brink of a fearful precipice, down which to fall was certain destruction. How beautiful had been his life-promise! How fair the opening day of his existence! Alas! the clouds were gathering already, and the low rumble of the distant thunder presaged the coming of a fearful tempest. Was there none to warn him of the danger? Alas! all might now come too late, for so few who enter the path in which his steps were treading will hearken to friendly counsel, or heed the solemn warning. Where was he now? This question recurred over and over again. He had left the bar-room with Judge Lyman and Green early in the evening, and had not made his appearance since. Who and what was Green? And Judge Lyman, was he a man of principle? One with whom it was safe to trust a youth like Willy Hammond?

While I mused thus, the bar-room door opened, and a man past the prime of life, with a somewhat florid face, which gave a strong relief to the gray, almost white hair that, suffered to grow freely, was pushed back, and lay in heavy masses on his coat collar, entered with a hasty step. He was almost venerable in appearance; yet, there was in his dark, quick eyes the brightness of unquenched loves, the fires of which were kindled at the altars of selfishness and sensuality. This I saw at a glance. There was a look of concern on his face, as he threw his eyes around the bar-room; and he seemed disappointed, I thought, at finding it empty.

"Is Simon Slade here?"

As I answered in the negative, Mrs. Slade entered through the door that opened from the yard, and stood behind the counter.

"Ah. Mrs. Slade! Good evening, madam!" he said.

"Good evening, Judge Hammond."

"Is your husband at home?"

"I believe he is," answered Mrs. Slade. "I think he's somewhere about the house."

"Ask him to step here, will you?"

Mrs. Slade went out. Nearly five minutes went by, during which time Judge Hammond paced the floor of the bar-room uneasily. Then the landlord made his appearance. The free, open, manly, self-satisfied expression of his countenance, which I had remarked on alighting from the stage in the afternoon, was gone. I noticed at once the change, for it was striking. He did not look steadily into the face of Judge Hammond, who asked him in a low voice, if his son had been there during the evening.

"He was here," said Slade.

"When?"

"He came in some time after dark and stayed, maybe, an hour."

"And hasn't been here since?"

"It's nearly two hours since he left the bar-room," replied the landlord.

Judge Hammond seemed perplexed. There was a degree of evasion in Slade's manner that he could hardly help noticing. To me it was all apparent, for I had lively suspicions that made my observation acute.

Judge Hammond crossed his arms behind him, and took three or four strides about the floor.

"Was Judge Lyman here to-night?" he then asked.

"He was," answered Slade.

"Did he and Willy go out together?"

The question seemed an unexpected one for the landlord. Slade appeared slightly confused, and did not answer promptly.

"I—I rather think they did," he said, after a brief hesitation.

"Ah, well! Perhaps he is at Judge Lyman's. I will call over there."

And Judge Hammond left the bar-room.

"Would you like to retire, sir?" said the landlord, now turning to me, with a forced smile—I saw that it was forced.

"If you please," I answered.

He lit a candle and conducted me to my room where, overwearied with the day's exertion, I soon fell asleep, and did not awake until the sun was shining brightly into my windows.

I remained at the village a portion of the day, but saw nothing of the parties in whom the incidents of the previous evening had awakened a lively interest. At four o'clock I left in the stage, and did not visit Cedarville again for a year.

—1854

Fanny Fern (Sara Willis Parton) 1811–1872

American novelist and journalist Fanny Fern was the first American woman to write a regular newspaper column. She was also the most highly paid newspaper writer of her time, man or woman. Her satirical writings, no-nonsense prose, and deft character sketches captivated readers on both sides of the Atlantic, making her one of the most well-known writers of the nineteenth century. Although she could write with heartfelt sincerity about human tragedy, she is primarily known today for her cynical and realistic undercutting of society's sacrosanct institutions. She wrote fearlessly on topics that were considered taboo for women writers at the time, and she pioneered in advocating the then-revolutionary concept of economic independence for women. She was also the originator of the saying, "The way to a man's heart is through his stomach."

The fifth of the nine children of Nathaniel and Hannah Willis of Boston, Sara was a spirited child, and her father—a converted Calvinist—sent her to a series of boarding schools in an attempt to curb her spirits and bring her to conversion. Although she did not succumb to her father's pressure on either count, she did obtain a good education. On May 4, 1837, she married Charles Eldredge. They had three daughters, one of whom died at the age of seven. Then, in October 1846, her husband died of typhoid fever. After his death, she was left without resources and with two children to support. Pressured into a loveless marriage with Samuel Farrington, a widower, she soon found that, as her daughter later said, the marriage was "a terrible mistake," and in January 1851 she left the abusive Farrington. Her family was scandalized and withheld financial assistance in an attempt to force her to return to her husband. She determined to earn her own living—as a seamstress or a teacher. Then, she tried writing short pieces for the newspapers. She appealed to her brother, Nathaniel Parker Willis, a well-known writer and editor, but he refused to help her. Finally, her first article was bought by a small Boston paper, *The Olive Branch*, and appeared on June 28, 1851. She published anonymously, and began using the pseudonym Fanny Fern. Soon, *The Olive Branch* and a second paper, the Boston *True Flag*, both of whose circulations had soared since they began publishing Fern's work, were willing to buy anything that she could write. Oliver Dyer, editor of the *New York Musical World and Times*, offered her a sizable increase in pay to write for him, and in 1853, publisher James Derby brought out a collection of her newspaper articles, *Fern Leaves From Fanny's Portfolio*, which became a bestseller. Fern moved to New York, and in 1855, her autobiographical novel, *Ruth Hall*, was published.

Fern's identity was revealed by an irate publisher whose exploitation of her had been revealed in *Ruth Hall*, and the novel, with its satiric treatment of her male relatives, caused a sensation as a *roman à clef*. Fern signed a contract with Robert Bonner of the *New York Ledger* to write a continuous story, "Fanny Ford," for one hundred dollars a column, and in January 1856—Farrington having divorced her in

1853—she married biographer James Parton, who was eleven years her junior. The couple signed a prenuptial agreement giving Fern sole possession of all her earnings. Later that year, she signed an exclusive contract with Bonner to write a weekly newspaper column, which she continued to do until her death in 1872.

Altogether, Fern published—in addition to her weekly newspaper columns—two novels (*Ruth Hall*, 1855, and *Rose Clark*, 1856), three children's books, and six collections of articles. For a modern reprint of her first novel and a hundred of her newspaper articles, see *Ruth Hall and Other Writings*, edited by Joyce W. Warren.

Further Reading Lauren Berlant, "The Female Woman: Fanny Fern and the Form of Sentiment," *The Culture of Sentiment: Race, Gender, and Sentimentality in Nineteenth-Century America*, ed. Shirley Samuels (1992); Susan K. Harris, "Inscribing and Defining: The Many Voices of Fanny Fern's *Ruth Hall*," *19ᵗʰ-Century American Women Writers: Interpretive Strategies* (1990); Joyce W. Warren, *Fanny Fern: An Independent Woman* (1992); Ann Douglas Wood, "The 'Scribbling Women' and Fanny Fern: Why Women Wrote," *American Quarterly* 23 (1971): 3–24.

—*Joyce W. Warren, Queens College, CUNY*

A Law More Nice than Just[1]

HERE I have been sitting twiddling the morning paper between my fingers this half hour, reflecting upon the following paragraph in it: "Emma Wilson was arrested yesterday for wearing man's apparel." Now, why this should be an actionable offense is past my finding out, or where's the harm in it, I am as much at a loss to see. Think of the old maids (and weep) who have to stay at home evening after evening, when, if they provided themselves with a coat, pants and hat, they might go abroad, instead of sitting there with their noses flattened against the window-pane, looking vainly for "the Coming Man." Think of the married women who stay at home after their day's toil is done, waiting wearily for their thoughtless, truant husbands, when they might be taking the much needed independent walk in trousers, which custom forbids to petticoats. And this, I fancy, may be the secret of this famous law—who knows? It *wouldn't* be pleasant for some of them to be surprised by a touch on the shoulder from some dapper young fellow, whose familiar treble voice belied his corduroys. That's it, now. What a fool I was not to think of it—not to remember that men who make the laws, make them to meet all these little emergencies.

Everybody knows what an everlasting drizzle of rain we have had lately, but nobody but a woman, and a woman who lives on fresh air and out-door exercise, knows the thraldom of taking her daily walk through a three weeks' rain, with skirts to hold up, and umbrella to hold down, and puddles to skip over, and gutters to walk

---

[1] **A Law More Nice than Just:** Refers to the laws that prohibited women from wearing pants in public.

round, and all the time in a fright lest, in an unguarded moment, her calves should become visible to some one of those rainy-day philanthropists who are interested in the public study of female anatomy.

One evening, after a long rainy day of scribbling, when my nerves were in double-twisted knots, and I felt as if myriads of little ants were leisurely traveling over me, and all for want of the walk which is my daily salvation, I stood at the window, looking at the slanting, persistent rain, and took my resolve: "*I'll do it*," said I, audibly, planting my slipper upon the carpet. "Do what?" asked Mr. Fern, looking up from a big book. "Put on a suit of your clothes and take a tramp with you," was the answer. "You dare not," was the rejoinder; "you are a little coward, only saucy on paper." It was the work of a moment, with such a challenge, to fly up stairs and overhaul my philosopher's wardrobe. Of course we had fun. Tailors must be a stingy set, I remarked, to be so sparing of their cloth, as I struggled into a pair of their handiwork, undeterred by the vociferous laughter of the wretch who had solemnly vowed to "cherish me" through all my tribulations. "Upon my word, everything seems to be narrow where it ought to be broad, and the waist of this coat might be made for a hogshead; and, ugh! this shirt collar is cutting my ears off, and you have not a decent cravat in the whole lot, and your vests are frights, and what am I to do with my hair?" Still no reply from Mr. Fern, who lay on the floor, faintly ejaculating, between his fits of laughter, "Oh, my! by Jove!—oh! by Jupiter!"

Was that to hinder me? Of course not. Strings and pins, women's never-failing resort, soon brought broadcloth and kerseymere to terms. I parted my hair on one side, rolled it under, and then secured it with hairpins; chose the best fitting coat, and cap-ping the climax with one of those soft, cosy hats, looked in the glass, where I beheld the very facsimile of a certain musical gentleman, whose photograph hangs this minute in Brady's entry.[2]

Well, Mr. Fern seized his hat, and out we went together. "Fanny," said he, "you must not take my arm; you are a fellow." "True," said I. "I forgot; and you must not help me over puddles, as you did just now, and do, for mercy's sake, stop laughing. There, there goes your hat—I mean *my* hat; confound the wind! and down comes my hair; lucky 'tis dark, isn't it?" But oh, the delicious freedom of that walk; after we were well started! No skirts to hold up, or to draggle their wet folds against my ankles; no stifling vail flapping in my face, and blinding my eyes; no umbrella to turn inside out, but instead, the cool rain driving slap into my face, and the resurrectionized blood coursing through my veins, and tingling in my cheeks. To be sure, Mr. Fern occasionally loitered behind, and leaned up against the side of a house to enjoy a little private "guffaw," and I could now and then hear a gasping "Oh, Fanny! Oh, my!" but none of these things moved me, and if I don't have a nicely-fitting suit of my own to wear rainy evenings, it is because—well, there are difficulties in the way. Who's the best tailor?

---

[2] **Brady's entry:** Refers to the photography studio of Mathew Brady.

Now, if any male or female Miss Nancy who reads this feels shocked, let 'em! Any woman who likes, may stay at home during a three weeks' rain, till her skin looks like parchment, and her eyes like those of a dead fish, or she may go out and get a consumption dragging round wet petticoats; I won't—I positively declare I won't. I shall begin *evenings* when *that* suit is made, and take private walking lessons with Mr. Fern, and they who choose may crook their backs at home for fashion, and then send for the doctor to straighten them; I prefer to patronize my shoe-maker and tailor. I've as good a right to preserve the healthy body God gave me, as if I were not a woman.

New York Ledger
July 10, 1858

A LAW MORE NICE THAN JUST

Number II

AFTER ALL, having tried it I affirm, that nothing reconciles a woman quicker to her feminity, than an experiment in male apparel, although I still maintain that she should not be forbidden by law to adopt it when necessity requires; at least, not till the practice is amended by which a female clerk, who performs her duty equally well with a male clerk, receives less salary, simply because she is a woman.

To have to jump on to the cars when in motion, and scramble yourself on to the platform as best you may without a helping hand; to be nudged roughly in the ribs by the conductor with, "your fare, sir?" to have your pretty little toes trod on, and no healing "beg your pardon," applied to the smart; to have all those nice-looking men who used to make you such crushing bows, and give you such insinuating smiles, pass you without the slightest interest in your coat tails, and perhaps push you against the wall or into the gutter, with a word tabooed by the clergy. In fine, to dispense with all those delicious little politenesses, (for men are great bears to each other,) to which one has been accustomed, and yet feel no inclination to take advantage of one's corduroys and secure an equivalent by making interest with the "fair sex," stale to you as a thrice-told tale. Isn't *that* a situation?

To be subject to the promptings of that unstifleable feminine desire for adornment, which is right and lovely within proper limits, and yet have no field for your operations. To have to conceal your silken hair, and yet be forbidden a becoming moustache, or whiskers, or beard—(all hail beards, I say!). To choke up your nice throat with a disguising cravat; to hide your bust (I trust no Miss Nancy is blushing) under a baggy vest. To have nobody ask you to ice cream, and yet be forbidden, by your horrible disgust of tobacco, to smoke. To have a gentleman ask you "the time sir?" when you are new to the geography of your watch-pocket. To accede to an invitation to test your "heft," by sitting down in one of those street-weighing chairs, and have one of the male bystanders, taking hold of your foot, remark, "Halloo, sir, you must not rest these upon the ground while you are being weighed;" and go grinning away in your coat-sleeve at your truly feminine faux pas.

And yet—and yet—to be able to step over the ferry-boat chain when you are in a distracted hurry, like any other fellow, without waiting for that tedious unhooking process, and quietly to enjoy your triumph over scores of impatient-waiting crushed petticoats behind you; to taste that nice lager beer "on draught;" to pick up contraband bits of science in a Medical Museum, forbidden to crinoline, and hold conversations with intelligent men, who supposing you to be a man, consequently talk sense to you. That is worth while.

Take it all in all, though, I thank the gods I am a woman. I had rather be loved than make love; though I could beat the makers of it, out and out, if I did not think it my duty to refrain out of regard to their feelings, and the final disappointment of the deluded women! But—oh, dear, I want to do such a quantity of "improper" things, that there is not the slightest real harm in doing. I want to see and know a thousand things which are forbidden to flounces—custom only can tell why—I can't. I want the free use of my ankles, for this summer at least, to take a journey; I want to climb and wade, and tramp about, without giving a thought to my clothes; without carrying about with me a long procession of trunks and boxes, which are the inevitable penalty of feminity as at present appareled. I hate a Bloomer, such as we have seen—words are weak to say how much; I hate myself as much in a man's dress; and yet I want to run my fingers through my cropped hair some fine morning without the bore of dressing it; put on some sort of loose blouse affair—it must be pretty, though—and a pair of Turkish trousers—*not* Bloomers—and a cap, or hat— and start; nary a trunk—"nary" a bandbox. Wouldn't that be fine? But propriety scowls and says, "ain't you ashamed of yourself, Fanny Fern?" *Yes, I am*, Miss Nancy. I *am* ashamed of myself, that I haven't the courage to carry out what would be so eminently convenient, and right, and proper under the circumstances. I am ashamed of myself that I sit like a fool on the piazza of some hotel every season, gazing at some distant mountain, which every pulse and muscle of my body, and every faculty of my soul, are urging me to climb, that I may "see the kingdoms of the earth and the glory of them." I *am* ashamed of myself that you, Miss Nancy, with your uplifted forefinger and your pursed-up mouth, should keep me out of a dress in which only I can hope to do such things. Can't I make a compromise with you, Miss Nancy? for I'm getting restless, as these lovely summer days pass on. I'd write you such long accounts of beautiful things, Miss Nancy—things which God made for female as well as male eyes to see; and I should come home so strong and healthy, Miss Nancy—a freckle or two, perhaps—but who cares? O-h-n-o-w, Miss Nancy, d-o—Pshaw! you cross old termagant! May Lucifer fly away wid ye.

New York Ledger
July 17, 1858

The Working-Girls of New York

NOWHERE more than in New York does the contest between squalor and splendor so sharply present itself. This is the first reflection of the observing stranger who walks its streets. Particularly is this noticeable with regard to its women. Jostling on the same pavement with the dainty fashionist is the care-worn working-girl. Looking at both these women, the question arises, which lives the more miserable life—she whom the world styles "fortunate," whose husband belongs to three clubs, and whose only meal with his family is an occasional breakfast, from year's end to year's end; who is as much a stranger to his own children as to the reader; whose young son of seventeen has already a detective on his track employed by his father to ascertain where and how he spends his nights and his father's money; swift retribution for that father who finds food, raiment, shelter, equipages for his household; but love, sympathy, companionship—never? Or she—this other woman—with a heart quite as hungry and unappeased, who also faces day by day the same appalling question: *Is this all life has for me?*

A great book is yet unwritten about women. Michelet has aired his wax-doll theories regarding them.[1] The defender of "woman's rights" has given us her views. Authors and authoresses of little, and big repute, have expressed themselves on this subject, and none of them as yet have begun to grasp it: men—because they lack spirituality, rightly and justly to interpret women; women—because they dare not, or will not tell us that which most interests us to know. Who shall write this bold, frank, truthful book remains to be seen. Meanwhile woman's millennium is yet a great way off; and while it slowly progresses, conservatism and indifference gaze through their spectacles at the seething elements of to-day, and wonder "what ails all our women?"

Let me tell you what ails the working-girls. While yet your breakfast is progressing, and your toilet unmade, comes forth through Chatham Street and the Bowery, a long procession of them by twos and threes to their daily labor. Their breakfast, so called, has been hastily swallowed in a tenement house, where two of them share, in a small room, the same miserable bed. Of its quality you may better judge, when you know that each of these girls pays but three dollars a week for board, to the working man and his wife where they lodge.

The room they occupy is close and unventilated, with no accommodations for personal cleanliness, and so near to the little Flinegans that their Celtic night-cries are distinctly heard. They have risen unrefreshed, as a matter of course, and their ill-cooked breakfast does not mend the matter. They emerge from the doorway

---

[1] **regarding them:** Jules Michelet (1798–1874), a French historian, claimed in works like *La femme* (1859) that the ideal woman was ignorant and passive.

where their passage is obstructed by "nanny goats" and ragged children rooting to-gether in the dirt, and pass out into the street. They shiver as the sharp wind of early morning strikes their temples. There is no look of youth on their faces; hard lines appear there. Their brows are knit; their eyes are sunken; their dress is flimsy, and foolish, and tawdry; always a hat, and feather or soiled artificial flower upon it; the hair dressed with an abortive attempt at style; a soiled petticoat; a greasy dress, a well-worn sacque or shawl, and a gilt breast-pin and earrings.

Now follow them to the large, black-looking building, where several hundred of them are manufacturing hoop-skirts. If you are a woman you have worn plenty; but you little thought what passed in the heads of these girls as their busy fingers glazed the wire, or prepared the spools for covering them, or secured the tapes which held them in their places. *You* could not stay five minutes in that room, where the noise of the machinery used is so deafening, that only by the motion of the lips could you comprehend a person speaking.

Five minutes! Why, these young creatures bear it, from seven in the morning till six in the evening; week after week, month after month, with only half an hour at midday to eat their dinner of a slice of bread and butter or an apple, which they usu-ally eat in the building, some of them having come a long distance. As I said, the roar of machinery in that room is like the roar of Niagara. Observe them as you enter. Not one lifts her head. They might as well be machines, for any interest or curiosity they show, save always to know *what o'clock it is*. Pitiful! pitiful, you almost sob to yourself, as you look at these young girls. *Young?* Alas! it is only in years that they are young.

Folly As It Flies

—1868

Elizabeth Cady Stanton 1815–1902

Known as one of the founders of the women's rights movement in America, Eliza-beth Cady Stanton dedicated over fifty years of her life to fighting for women's suf-frage and equal treatment under the law. She was born in 1815 in Johnstown, New York. Cady Stanton's father was a lawyer, judge, and congressman. While he openly expressed his belief in male superiority, Daniel Cady also provided an excellent edu-cation for his daughter, one few women were able to obtain at the time. Formal schooling, in addition to the time she spent in her father's law office exploring laws she felt were unfair to women, became the groundwork for Cady Stanton's future activism. She married abolitionist Henry Stanton in 1839. Their wedding ceremony did not include the word "obey," at Cady Stanton's insistence. The couple's somewhat unusual honeymoon found them at the World's Anti-Slavery Convention in London, where Cady Stanton met Lucretia Mott and the two women first discussed holding a convention dedicated to the rights of women. By 1847, Cady Stanton had three children (she would eventually have seven), and the family moved to Seneca Falls, New York, on account of Henry Stanton's poor health.

In July of 1848, Cady Stanton, in conjunction with Lucretia Mott and other early suffragettes, organized the First Woman's Rights convention held in Seneca Falls. The famous "Declaration of Sentiments" was issued during this convention. Modeled after the Declaration of Independence, the document outlined eighteen points of contestation between women and the law and society and called for the equal treatment of men and women. Despite widespread public opposition to the convention and to women's rights in general, many similar conventions followed and Cady Stanton became a tireless crusader for the cause. From 1868 to 1870, Cady Stanton teamed with Susan B. Anthony to publish the *Revolution*, a women's rights newspaper advocating suffrage; the paper displayed the motto "Principle, not Policy; Justice, not Favors; Men, their rights and & nothing more; Women, their rights & nothing less" on its front page. In 1869, Cady Stanton formed the National Woman Suffrage Association, which would later merge (in 1890) with the more conservative American Woman Suffrage Association to become the National American Woman Suffrage Association.

Along with Anthony and Matilda Joslyn Gage, Cady Stanton collaborated and edited three volumes of the *History of Woman Suffrage*, which chronicled the years 1848–1877 within the movement. In 1898, she published her autobiography, *Eighty Years and More*. Cady Stanton died in 1902 at the age of eighty-six. Eighteen years later, in 1920, the Nineteenth Amendment gave women the right to vote—a victory for the women's rights movement that owed much to Cady Stanton and her unyielding efforts as an activist, writer, and lecturer.

Declaration of Sentiments

When, in the course of human events, it becomes necessary for one portion of the family of man to assume among the people of the earth a position different from that which they have hitherto occupied, but one to which the laws of nature and of nature's God entitle them, a decent respect to the opinions of mankind requires that they should declare the causes that impel them to such a course.

We hold these truths to be self-evident: that all men and women are created equal; that they are endowed by their Creator with certain inalienable rights; that among these are life, liberty, and the pursuit of happiness; that to secure these rights governments are instituted, deriving their just powers from the consent of the governed. Whenever any form of government becomes destructive of these ends, it is the right of those who suffer from it to refuse allegiance to it, and to insist upon the institution of a new government, laying its foundation on such principles, and organizing its powers in such form, as to them shall seem most likely to effect their safety and happiness. Prudence, indeed, will dictate that governments long established should not be changed for light and transient causes; and accordingly all experience hath shown that mankind are more disposed to suffer, while evils are sufferable, than to right themselves by abolishing the forms to which they were accustomed. But when a long train of abuses and usurpations, pursuing invariably the same object evinces a design to reduce them under absolute despotism, it is their duty to throw off such government, and to provide new guards for their future security. Such has been the patient sufferance of the women under this government, and such is now the necessity which constrains them to demand the equal station to which they are entitled.

The history of mankind is a history of repeated injuries and usurpations on the part of man toward woman, having in direct object the establishment of an absolute tyranny over her. To prove this, let facts be submitted to a candid world.

He has never permitted her to exercise her inalienable right to the elective franchise.

He has compelled her to submit to laws, in the formation of which she had no voice.

He has withheld from her rights which are given to the most ignorant and degraded men—both natives and foreigners.

Having deprived her of this first right of a citizen, the elective franchise, thereby leaving her without representation in the halls of legislation, he has oppressed her on all sides.

He has made her, if married, in the eye of the law, civilly dead.

He has taken from her all right in property, even to the wages she earns.

He has made her, morally, an irresponsible being, as she can commit many crimes with impunity, provided they be done in the presence of her husband. In the covenant of marriage, she is compelled to promise obedience to her husband, he becoming, to all intents and purposes, her master—the law giving him power to deprive her of her liberty, and to administer chastisement.

He has so framed the laws of divorce, as to what shall be the proper causes, and in case of separation, to whom the guardianship of the children shall be given, as to be wholly regardless of the happiness of women—the law, in all cases, going upon a false supposition of the supremacy of man, and giving all power into his hands.

After depriving her of all rights as a married woman, if single, and the owner of property, he has taxed her to support a government which recognizes her only when her property can be made profitable to it.

He has monopolized nearly all the profitable employments, and from those she is permitted to follow, she receives but a scanty remuneration. He closes against her all the avenues to wealth and distinction which he considers most honorable to himself. As a teacher of theology, medicine, or law, she is not known.

He has denied her the facilities for obtaining a thorough education, all colleges being closed against her.

He allows her in Church, as well as State, but a subordinate position, claiming Apostolic authority for her exclusion from the ministry, and, with some exceptions, from any public participation in the affairs of the Church.

He has created a false public sentiment by giving to the world a different code of morals for men and women, by which moral delinquencies which exclude women from society, are not only tolerated, but deemed of little account in man.

He has usurped the prerogative of Jehovah himself, claiming it as his right to assign for her a sphere of action, when that belongs to her conscience and to her God.

He has endeavored, in every way that he could, to destroy her confidence in her own powers, to lessen her self-respect, and to make her willing to lead a dependent and abject life.

Now, in view of this entire disfranchisement of one half the people of this country, their social and religious degradation in view of the unjust laws above mentioned, and because women do feel themselves aggrieved, oppressed, and fraudulently deprived of their most sacred rights, we insist that they have immediate admission to all the rights and privileges which belong to them as citizens of the United States.

In entering upon the great work before us, we anticipate no small amount of misconception, misrepresentation, and ridicule, but we shall use every instrumentality within our power to effect our object. We shall employ agents, circulate tracts, petition the State and National legislatures, and endeavor to enlist the pulpit and the press in our behalf. We hope this Convention will be followed by a series of Conventions embracing every part of the country.

The following resolutions were discussed by Lucretia Mott, Thomas and Mary Ann McClintock, Amy Post, Catharine A. F. Stebbins, and others, and were adopted.

WHEREAS, The great precept of nature is conceded to be, that "man shall pursue his own true and substantial happiness." Blackstone in his Commentaries remarks, that this law of Nature being coeval with mankind, and dictated by God himself, is of course superior in obligation to any other. It is binding over all the globe, in all countries and at all times; no human laws are of any validity if contrary to this, and such of them as are valid, derive all their force, and all their validity, and all their authority, mediately and immediately, from this original; therefore,

Resolved, That such laws as conflict, in any way, with the true and substantial happiness of woman, are contrary to the great precept of nature and of no validity, for this is "superior in obligation to any other."

Resolved, That all laws which prevent woman from occupying such a station in society as her conscience shall dictate, or which place her in a position inferior to that of man, are contrary to the great precept of nature, and therefore of no force or authority.

Resolved, That woman is man's equal—was intended to be so by the Creator, and the highest good of the race demands that she should be recognized as such.

Resolved, That the women of this country ought to be enlightened in regard to the laws under which they live, that they may no longer publish their degradation by declaring themselves satisfied with their present position, nor their ignorance, by asserting that they have all the rights they want.

Resolved, That inasmuch as man, while claiming for himself intellectual superiority, does accord to woman moral superiority, it is pre-eminently his duty to encourage her to speak, and teach, as she has an opportunity, in all religious assemblies.

Resolved, That the same amount of virtue, delicacy, and refinement of behavior that is required of woman in the social state, should also be required of man, and the same transgressions should be visited with equal severity on both man and woman.

Resolved, That the objection of indelicacy and impropriety, which is so often brought against woman when she addresses a public audience, comes with a very ill-grace from those who encourage, by their attendance, her appearance on the stage, in the concert, or in feats of the circus.

Resolved, That woman has too long rested satisfied in the circumscribed limits which corrupt customs and a perverted application of the Scriptures have marked out for her, and that it is time she should move in the enlarged sphere which her great Creator has assigned her.

Resolved, That it is the duty of the women of this country to secure to themselves their sacred right to the elective franchise.

Resolved, That the equality of human rights results necessarily from the fact of the identity of the race in capabilities and responsibilities.

Resolved, therefore, That, being invested by the Creator with the same capabilities, and the same consciousness of responsibility for their exercise, it is demonstrably the right and duty of woman, equally with man, to promote every righteous cause by every righteous means; and especially in regard to the great subjects of morals and religion, it is self-evidently her right to participate with her brother in teaching them, both in private and in public, by writing and by speaking, by any instrumentalities proper to be used, and in any assemblies proper to be held; and this being a self-evident truth growing out of the divinely implanted principles of human nature, any custom or authority adverse to it, whether modern or wearing the hoary sanction of antiquity, is to be regarded as a self-evident falsehood, and at war with mankind:

At the last session. Lucretia Mott offered and spoke to the following resolution:
Resolved, That the speedy success of our cause depends upon the zealous and untiring efforts of both men and women, for the overthrow of the monopoly of the pulpit, and for the securing to woman an equal participation with men in the various trades, professions, and commerce.

The only resolution that was not unanimously adopted was the ninth, urging the women of the country to secure to themselves the elective franchise. Those who took part in the debate feared a demand for the right to vote would defeat others they deemed more rational, and make the whole movement ridiculous.

But Mrs. Stanton and Frederick Douglass seeing that the power to choose rulers and make laws, was the right by which all others could be secured, persistently advocated the resolution, and at last carried it by a small majority.

Thus it will be seen that the Declaration and resolutions in the very first Convention, demanded all the most radical friends of the movement have since claimed—such as equal rights in the universities, in the trades and professions; the right to vote; to share in all political offices, honors, and emoluments; to complete equality in marriage, to personal freedom, property, wages, children; to make contracts; to sue, and be sued; and to testify in courts of justice. At this time the condition of married women, under the Common Law, was nearly as degraded as that of the slave on the Southern plantation. The Convention continued through two entire days, and late into the evenings. The deepest interest was manifested to its close.

The proceedings were extensively published, unsparingly ridiculed by the press, and denounced by the pulpit, much to the surprise and chagrin of the leaders. Being deeply in earnest, and believing their demands pre-eminently wise and just, they were wholly unprepared to find themselves the target for the jibes and jeers of the nation. The Declaration was signed by one hundred men, and women, *many of whom* withdrew their names as soon as the storm of ridicule began to break. The comments of the press were carefully preserved, and it is curious to see that the same old arguments, and objections rife at the start, are reproduced by the press.

—1848

Ik Marvel (Donald Grant Mitchell) 1822–1908

Despite the immense popularity of two of his early novels, *Reveries of a Bachelor: or, A Book of the Heart* (1850) and *Dream Life: A Fable of the Seasons* (1851) both written under the pseudonym Ik Marvel, Donald Grant Mitchell remains a largely

H. N. Roberts, *Francis Wayland Sherman at the Age of 2 Years 10 Months*, 1862 [Albumen print from wet collodion negative, 18.6x13.3 cm] By capturing the moment of childhood in connection with a favorite toy, this early photograph presents an idyllic memory of a middle class child.
© *The Cleveland Museum of Art, John L. Severance Fund 2002.34.*

unstudied literary figure. Mitchell took farming and the rural life in general as his subject matter, and his work found resonance with a nineteenth-century audience that favored sentimentality. Mitchell was born in 1822 in Norwich, Connecticut and was sent to a rigorous boarding school as a youth. He later attended Yale University, where he was an editor of the *Yale Literary Magazine*, and graduated in 1841. Mitchell became known as a satirist in the late 1840s after he published letters called "Capitol Sketches" in the *New York Courier and Enquirer* that discussed the time he spent in Washington D.C. It was *Reveries of a Bachelor*, however, that brought him fame. Upon its publication in 1850, the work sold fourteen thousand copies the first year—an astronomical first run. The sentimental narrative follows the shifting thoughts of an everyman bachelor as he contemplates first the joys of bachelorhood and then the satisfactions of married life. The popularity of this tale is indicative of the draw of the sentimental to a nineteenth-century audience. The success of *Reveries* led to the publication of a sequel, *Dream Life: A Fable of the Seasons* in 1851, which revisited much of Mitchell's sentimental territory. During the Civil War, Mitchell's writing turned to agrarian themes and topics, but his later work never again attained the acclaim of *Reveries*. Mitchell died in 1908.

From Reveries of a Bachelor

FIRST REVERIE: SMOKE, FLAME AND ASHES

OVER A WOOD FIRE.

I HAVE got a quiet farmhouse in the country, a very humble place to be sure, tenanted by a worthy enough man, of the old New-England stamp, where I sometimes go for a day or two in the winter, to look over the farm-accounts, and to see how the stock is thriving on the winter's keep.

One side the door, as you enter from the porch, is a little parlor, scarce twelve feet by ten, with a cosy looking fire-place—a heavy oak floor—a couple of arm chairs and a brown table with carved lions' feet. Out of this room opens a little cabinet, only big enough for a broad bachelor bedstead, where I sleep upon feathers, and wake in the morning, with my eye upon a saucy colored, lithographic print of some fancy "Bessy."

It happens to be the only house in the world, of which I am *bona-fide* owner; and I take a vast deal of comfort in treating it just as I choose. I manage to break some article of furniture, almost every time I pay it a visit; and if I cannot open the window readily of a morning, to breathe the fresh air, I knock out a pane or two of glass with my boot. I lean against the walls in a very old arm-chair there is on the premises, and scarce ever fail to worry such a hole in the plastering, as would set me down for a round charge for damages in town, or make a prim housewife fret herself into a raging fever. I laugh out loud with myself, in my big arm-chair, when I think that I am neither afraid of one nor the other.

As for the fire, I keep the little hearth so hot, as to warm half the cellar below, and the whole space between the jams, roars for hours together, with white flame. To be sure the windows are not very tight, between broken panes, and bad joints, so that the fire, large as it is, is by no means an extravagant comfort.

As night approaches, I have a huge pile of oak and hickory placed beside the hearth; I put out the tallow candle on the mantel, (using the family snuffers, with one leg broke,)—then, drawing my chair directly in front of the blazing wood, and setting one foot on each of the old iron fire-dogs, (until they grow too warm,) I dispose myself for an evening of such sober, and thoughtful quietude, as I believe, on my soul, that very few of my fellow-men have the good fortune to enjoy.

My tenant meantime, in the other room, I can hear now and then,—though there is a thick stone chimney, and broad entry between,—multiplying contrivances with his wife, to put two babies to sleep. This occupies them, I should say, usually an hour; though my only measure of time, (for I never carry a watch into the country,) is the blaze of my fire. By ten, or thereabouts, my stock of wood is nearly exhausted; I pile upon the hot coals what remains, and sit watching how it kindles, and blazes, and goes out,—even like our joys!—and then, slip by the light of the embers into my bed, where I luxuriate in such sound, and healthful slumber, as only such rattling window frames, and country air, can supply.

But to return: the other evening—it happened to be on my last visit to my farm-house—when I had exhausted all the ordinary rural topics of thought, had formed all sorts of conjectures as to the income of the year; had planned a new wall around one lot, and the clearing up of another, now covered with patriarchal wood; and wondered if the little ricketty house would not be after all a snug enough box, to live and to die in—I fell on a sudden into such an unprecedented line of thought, which took such deep hold of my sympathies—sometimes even starting tears—that I determined, the next day, to set as much of it as I could recall, on paper.

Something—it may have been the home-looking blaze, (I am a bachelor of—say six and twenty,) or possibly a plaintive cry of the baby in my tenant's room, had suggested to me the thought of—Marriage.

I piled upon the heated fire-dogs, the last arm-full of my wood; and now, said I, bracing myself courageously between the arms of my chair,—I'll not flinch;—I'll pursue the thought wherever it leads, though it lead me to the d—(I am apt to be hasty,)—at least—continued I, softening,—until my fire is out.

The wood was green, and at first showed no disposition to blaze. It smoked furiously. Smoke, thought I, always goes before blaze; and so does doubt go before decision: and my Reverie, from that very starting point, slipped into this shape:—

I.

Smoke—Signifying Doubt.

A WIFE?—thought I;—yes, a wife!

And why!

And pray, my dear sir, why not—why? Why not doubt; why not hesitate; why not tremble?

Does a man buy a ticket in a lottery—a poor man, whose whole earnings go in to secure the ticket,—without trembling, hesitating, and doubting?

Can a man stake his bachelor respectability, his independence, and comfort, upon the die of absorbing, unchanging, relentless marriage, without trembling at the venture?

Shall a man who has been free to chase his fancies over the wide-world, without lett or hindrance shut himself up to marriage-ship, within four walls called Home, that are to claim him, his time, his trouble, and his tears, thenceforward forever more, without doubts thick, and thick-coming as Smoke?

Shall he who has been hitherto a mere observer of other men's cares and business—moving off where they made him sick of heart, approaching whenever and wherever they made him gleeful—shall he now undertake administration of just such cares and business, without qualms? Shall he, whose whole life has been but a nimble succession of escapes from trifling difficulties, now broach without doubtings—that Matrimony, where if difficulty beset him, there is no escape? Shall this brain of mine, careless-working, never tired with idleness, feeding on long vagaries, and high, gigantic castles, dreaming out beatitudes hour by hour— turn itself at length to such dull task-work, as thinking out a livelihood for wife and children?

Where thenceforward will be those sunny dreams, in which I have warmed my fancies, and my heart, and lighted my eye with crystal? This very marriage, which a brilliant working imagination has invested time and again with brightness, and delight, can serve no longer as a mine for teeming fancy: all, alas, will be gone— reduced to the dull standard of the actual! No more room for intrepid forays of imagination—no more gorgeous realm-making—all will be over!

Why not, I thought, go on dreaming?

Can any wife be prettier than an after dinner fancy, idle and yet vivid, can paint for you? Can any children make less noise, than the little rosy-cheeked ones, who have no existence, except in the *omnium gatherum* of your own brain? Can any housewife be more unexceptionable than she who goes sweeping daintily the cobwebs that gather in your dreams? Can any domestic larder be better stocked, than the private larder of your head dozing on a cushioned chair-back at Delmonico's? Can any family purse be better filled than the exceeding plump one, you dream of, after reading such pleasant books as Munchausen, or Typee?

But if, after all, it must be—duty, or what-not, making provocation—what then? And I clapped my feet hard against the fire-dogs, and leaned back, and turned my face to the ceiling, as much as to say;—And where on earth, then, shall a poor devil look for a wife?

Somebody says, Lyttleton or Shaftesbury I think, that "marriages would be happier if they were all arranged by the Lord Chancellor." Unfortunately, we have no Lord Chancellor to make this commutation of our misery.

Shall a man then scour the country on a mule's back, like Honest Gil Blas of Santillane; or shall he make application to some such intervening providence as Madame St. Mare, who, as I see by the Presse, manages these matters to one's hand, for some five percent. on the fortunes of the parties?

I have trouted, when the brook was so low, and the sky so hot, that I might as well have thrown my fly upon the turnpike; and I have hunted hare at noon, and wood-cock in snow-time—never despairing, scarce doubting; but for a poor hunter of his kind, without traps or snares, or any aid of police or constabulary, to traverse the world, where are swarming, on a moderate computation, some three hundred and odd millions of unmarried women, for a single capture—irremediable, unchangeable—and yet a capture which by strange metonymy, not laid down in the books, is very apt to turn captor into captive, and make game of hunter—all this, surely, surely may make a man shrug with doubt!

Then—again,—there are the plaguey wife's-relations. Who knows how many third, fourth, or fifth cousins will appear at careless complimentary intervals, long after you had settled into the placid belief that all congratulatory visits were at an end! How many twisted headed brothers will be putting in their advice, as a friend to Peggy?

How many maiden aunts will come to spend a month or two with their "dear Peggy," and want to know every tea-time, "if she isn't a dear love of a wife?" Then, dear father-in-law will beg, (taking dear Peggy's hand in his,) to give a little wholesome counsel; and will be very sure to advise just the contrary of what you had determined to undertake. And dear mamma-in-law must set her nose into Peggy's cupboard, and insist upon having the key to your own private locker in the wainscot.

Then, perhaps, there is a little bevy of dirty-nosed nephews who come to spend the holydays, and eat up your East India sweetmeats; and who are forever tramping over your head, or raising the old Harry below, while you are busy with your clients. Last, and worst, is some fidgety old uncle, forever too cold or too hot, who vexes you with his patronizing airs, and impudently kisses his little Peggy!

———That could be borne, however: for perhaps he has promised his fortune to Peggy. Peggy, then, will be rich:—(and the thought made me rub my shins, which were now getting comfortably warm upon the fire-dogs.) Then, she will be forever talking of *her* fortune; and pleasantly reminding you on occasion of a favorite purchase,—how lucky that *she* had the means; and dropping hints about economy; and buying very extravagant Paisleys.

She will annoy you by looking over the stock-list at breakfast time; and mention quite carelessly to your clients, that she is interested in *such*, or such a speculation.

She will be provokingly silent when you hint to a tradesman, that you have not the money by you, for his small bill;—in short, she will tear the life out of you, making you pay in righteous retribution of annoyance, grief, vexation, shame, and sickness of heart, for the superlative folly of "marrying rich."

———But if not rich, then poor. Bah! the thought made me stir the coals; but there was still no blaze. The paltry earnings you are able to wring out of clients by the sweat of your brow, will now be all *our* income; you will be pestered for pin-money, and pestered with your poor wife's-relations. Ten to one, she will stickle about taste—"Sir Visto's"—and want to make this so pretty, and that so charming, if she *only* had the means; and is sure Paul (a kiss) can't deny his little Peggy such a trifling sum, and all for the common benefit.

Then she, for one, means that *her* children shan't go a begging for clothes,—and another pull at the purse. Trust a poor mother to dress her children in finery!

Perhaps she is ugly;—not noticeable at first; but growing on her, and (what is worse) growing faster on you. You wonder why you didn't see that vulgar nose long ago: and that lip—it is very strange, you think, that you ever thought it pretty. And then,—to come to breakfast, with her hair looking as it does, and you, not so much as daring to say—"Peggy, *do* brush your hair!" Her foot too—not very bad when decently *chaussée*—but now since she's married, she does wear such infernal slippers! And yet for all this, to be prigging up for an hour, when any of my old chums come to dine with me!

"Bless your kind hearts! my dear fellows," said I, thrusting the tongs into the coals, and speaking out loud, as if my voice could reach from Virginia to Paris—"not married yet!"

Perhaps Peggy is pretty enough—only shrewish.

———No matter for cold coffee;—you should have been up before.

What sad, thin, poorly cooked chops, to eat with your rolls!

———She thinks they are very good, and wonders how you can set such an example to your children.

The butter is nauseating.

——She has no other, and hopes you'll not raise a storm about butter a little turned.—I think I see myself—ruminated I—sitting meekly at table, scarce daring to lift up my eyes, utterly fagged out with some quarrel of yesterday, choking down detestably sour muffins, that my wife thinks are "delicious"—slipping in dried mouthfuls of burnt ham off the side of my fork tines,—slipping off my chair side-ways at the end, and slipping out with my hat between my knees, to business, and never feeling myself a competent, sound-minded man, till the oak door is between me and Peggy!

—"Ha, ha,—not yet!" said I; and in so earnest a tone, that my dog started to his feet—cocked his eye to have a good look into my face—met my smile of triumph with an amiable wag of the tail, and curled up again in the corner.

Again, Peggy is rich enough, well enough, mild enough, only she doesn't care a fig for you. She has married you because father, or grandfather thought the match eligible, and because she didn't wish to disoblige them. Besides, she didn't positively hate you, and thought you were a respectable enough young person;—she has told you so repeatedly at dinner. She wonders you like to read poetry; she wishes you would buy her a good cook-book; and insists upon your making your will at the birth of the first baby.

She thinks Captain So-and-So a splendid looking fellow, and wishes you would trim up a little, were it only for appearance' sake.

You need not hurry up from the office so early at night:—she, bless her dear heart!—does not feel lonely. You read to her a love tale; she interrupts the pathetic parts with directions to her seamstress. You read of marriages: she sighs, and asks if Captain So-and-So has left town! She hates to be mewed up in a cottage, or between brick walls; she does *so* love the Springs!

But, again, Peggy loves you;—at least she swears it, with her hand on the Sor-rows of Werter. She has pin-money which she spends for the Literary World, and the Friends in Council. She is not bad looking, save a bit too much of forehead; nor is she sluttish, unless a *negligé* till three o'clock, and an ink stain on the fore finger be sluttish;—but then she is such a sad blue!

You never fancied when you saw her buried in a three volume novel, that it was anything more than a girlish vagary; and when she quoted Latin, you thought in-nocently, that she had a capital memory for her samplers.

But to be bored eternally about Divine Danté and funny Goldoni, is too bad. Your copy of Tasso, a treasure print of 1680, is all bethumbed and dogs-eared, and spotted with baby gruel. Even your Seneca—an Elzevir—is all sweaty with handling. She adores La Fontaine, reads Balzac with a kind of artist-scowl, and will not let Greek alone.

You hint at broken rest and an aching head at breakfast, and she will fling you a scrap of Anthology—in lieu of the camphor bottle—or chant the αἰαῖ αἰαῖ, of tragic chorus.

——The nurse is getting dinner; you are holding the baby; Peggy is reading Bruyère.

The fire smoked thick as pitch, and puffed out little clouds over the chimney piece. I gave the fore-stick a kick, at the thought of Peggy, baby, and Bruyère.

——Suddenly the flame flickered bluely athwart the smoke—caught at a twig below—rolled round the mossy oak-stick—twined among the crackling tree-limbs—mounted—lit up the whole body of smoke, and blazed out cheerily and bright. Doubt vanished with Smoke, and Hope began with Flame.

II.

Blaze—Signifying Cheer.

I PUSHED my chair back; drew up another; stretched out my feet cosily upon it, rested my elbows on the chair arms, leaned my head on one hand, and looked straight into the leaping, and dancing flame.

——Love is a flame—ruminated I; and (glancing round the room) how a flame brightens up a man's habitation.

"Carlo," said I, calling up my dog into the light, "good fellow, Carlo!" and I patted him kindly, and he wagged his tail, and laid his nose across my knee, and looked wistfully up in my face; then strode away,—turned to look again, and lay down to sleep.

"Pho, the brute!" said I, "it is not enough after all, to like a dog."

——If now in that chair yonder, not the one your feet lie upon, but the other, beside you—closer yet—were seated a sweet-faced girl, with a pretty little foot lying out upon the hearth—a bit of lace running round the swelling throat—the hair parted to a charm over a forehead fair as any of your dreams;—and if you could reach an arm around that chair back, without fear of giving offence, and suffer your fingers to play idly with those curls that escape down the neck; and if you could clasp with your other hand those little white, taper fingers of hers, which lie so temptingly within reach,—and so, talk softly and low in presence of the blaze, while the hours slip without knowledge, and the winter winds whistle uncared for;—if, in short, you were no bachelor, but the husband of some such sweet image—(dream, call it rather,) would it not be far pleasanter than this cold single night-sitting—counting the sticks—reckoning the length of the blaze, and the height of the falling snow?

And if, some or all of those wild vagaries that grow on your fancy at such an hour, you could whisper into listening, because loving ears—ears not tired with listening, because it is you who whisper—ears ever indulgent because eager to praise;—and if your darkest fancies were lit up, not merely with bright wood fire, but with a ringing laugh of that sweet face turned up in fond rebuke—how far better, than to be waxing black, and sour, over pestilential humors—alone—your very dog asleep!

And if when a glowing thought comes into your brain, quick and sudden, you could tell it over as to a second self, to that sweet creature, who is not away, because she loves to be there; and if you could watch the thought catching that girlish mind, illuming that fair brow, sparkling in those pleasantest of eyes—how far better than to feel it slumbering, and going out, heavy, lifeless, and dead, in your own selfish fancy. And if a generous emotion steals over you—coming, you know not whither, would there not be a richer charm in lavishing it in caress, or endearing word, upon that fondest, and most dear one, than in patting your glossy coated dog, or sinking lonely to smiling slumbers?

How would not benevolence ripen with such monitor to task it! How would not selfishness grow faint and dull, leaning ever to that second self, which is the loved one! How would not guile shiver, and grow weak, before that girl-brow, and eye of innocence! How would not all that boyhood prized of enthusiasm, and quick blood, and life, renew itself in such presence!

The fire was getting hotter, and I moved into the middle of the room. The shadows the flames made, were playing like fairy forms over floor, and wall, and ceiling.

My fancy would surely quicken, thought I, if such being were in attendance. Surely imagination would be stronger, and purer, if it could have the playful fancies of dawning womanhood to delight it. All toil would be torn from mind-labor, if but another heart grew into this present soul, quickening it, warming it, cheering it, bidding it ever,—God speed!

Her face would make a halo, rich as a rainbow, atop of all such noisome things, as we lonely souls call trouble. Her smile would illumine the blackest of crowding cares; and darkness that now seats you despondent, in your solitary chair for days together, weaving bitter fancies, dreaming bitter dreams, would grow light and thin, and spread, and float away,—chased by that beloved smile.

Your friend—poor fellow!—dies:—never mind, that gentle clasp of *her* fingers, as she steals behind you, telling you not to weep—it is worth ten friends!

Your sister, sweet one, is dead—buried. The worms are busy with all her fairness. How it makes you think earth nothing but a spot to dig graves upon!

——It is more: *she* she says, will be a sister; and the waving curls as she leans upon your shoulder, touch your cheek, and your wet eye turns to meet those other eyes——God has sent his angel, surely!

Your mother, alas for it, she is gone! Is there any bitterness to a youth, alone, and homeless, like this!

But you are not homeless; you are not alone: *she* is there;—her tears softening yours, her smile lighting yours, her grief killing yours; and you live again, to assuage that kind sorrow of hers.

Then—those children, rosy, fair-haired; no, they do not disturb you with their prattle now—they are yours! Toss away there on the green-sward—never mind the hyacinths, the snowdrops, the violets, if so be any are there; the perfume of their healthful lips is worth all the flowers of the world. No need now to gather wild bouquets to love, and cherish: flower, tree, gun, are all dead things; things livelier hold your soul.

And she, the mother, sweetest and fairest of all, watching, tending, caressing, loving, till your own heart grows pained with tenderest jealousy, and cures itself with loving.

You have no need now of any cold lecture to teach thankfulness: your heart is full of it. No need now, as once, of bursting blossoms, of trees taking leaf, and greenness, to turn thought kindly, and thankfully; for ever, beside you, there is bloom, and ever beside you there is fruit,—for which eye, heart, and soul are full of unknown, and unspoken, because unspeakable, thank-offering.

And if sickness catches you, binds you, lays you down—no lonely moanings, and wicked curses at careless stepping nurses. *The* step is noiseless, and yet distinct beside you. The white curtains are drawn, or withdrawn by the magic of that other presence; and the soft, cool hand is upon your brow.

No cold comfortings of friend-watchers, merely come in to steal a word away from that outer world which is pulling at their skirts; but, ever, the sad, shaded brow of her, whose lightest sorrow for your sake is your greatest grief,—if it were not a greater joy.

The blaze was leaping light and high, and the wood falling under the growing heat.

——So, continued I, this heart would be at length itself;—striving with everything gross, even now as it clings to grossness. Love would make its strength native and progressive. Earth's cares would fly. Joys would double. Susceptibilities be quickened; Love master self; and having made the mastery, stretch onward, and upward toward Infinitude.

And if the end came, and sickness brought that follower—Great Follower—which sooner or later is sure to come after, then the heart, and the hand of Love, ever near, are giving to your tired soul, daily and hourly, lessons of that love which consoles, which triumphs, which circleth all, and centereth in all—Love Infinite, and Divine!

Kind hands—none but *hers*—will smooth the hair upon your brow as the chill grows damp, and heavy on it; and her fingers—none but hers—will lie in yours as the wasted flesh stiffens, and hardens for the ground. *Her* tears,—you could feel no others, if oceans fell—will warm your drooping features once more to life; once more your eye lighted in joyous triumph, kindle in her smile, and then——

The fire fell upon the hearth; the blaze gave a last leap—a flicker—then another—caught a little remaining twig—blazed up—wavered—went out.

There was nothing but a bed of glowing embers, over which the white ashes gathered fast. I was alone, with only my dog for company.

III.

Ashes—Signifying Desolation

After all, thought I, ashes follow blaze, inevitably as Death follows Life. Misery treads on the heels of Joy; Anguish rides swift after Pleasure.

"Come to me again, Carlo," said I, to my dog; and I patted him fondly once more, but now only by the light of the dying embers.

It is very little pleasure one takes in fondling brute favorites; but it is a pleasure that when it passes, leaves no void. It is only a little alleviating redundance in your solitary heart-life, which if lost, another can be supplied.

But if your heart, not solitary—not quieting its humors with mere love of chase, or dog—not repressing year after year, its earnest yearnings after something better, and more spiritual,—has fairly linked itself by bonds strong as life, to another heart—is the casting off easy, then?

Is it then only a little heart-redundancy cut off, which the next bright sunset will fill up?

And my fancy, as it had painted doubt under the smoke, and cheer under warmth of the blaze, so now it began under the faint light of the smouldering embers, to picture heart-desolation.

——What kind congratulatory letters, hosts of them, coming from old and half-forgotten friends, now that your happiness is a year, or two years old!

"Beautiful."

——Aye to be sure beautiful!

"Rich."

——Pho, the dawdler! how little he knows of heart-treasure, who speaks of wealth to a man who loves his wife, as a wife only should be loved!

"Young."

——Young indeed; guileless as infancy; charming as the morning.

Ah, these letters bear a sting: they bring to mind, with new, and newer freshness, if it be possible, the value of that, which you tremble lest you lose.

How anxiously you watch that step—if it lose not its buoyancy; How you study the color on that cheek, if it grow not fainter; How you tremble at the lustre in those eyes, if it be not the lustre of Death, How you totter under the weight of that muslin sleeve—a phantom weight! How you fear to do it, and yet press forward, to note if that breathing be quickened, as you ascend the home-heights, to look off on sunset lighting the plain.

Is your sleep, quiet sleep, after that she has whispered to you her fears, and in the same breath—soft as a sigh, sharp as an arrow—bid you bear it bravely?

Perhaps,—the embers were now glowing fresher, a little kindling, before the ashes—she triumphs over disease.

But, Poverty, the world's almoner, has come to you with ready, spare hand.

Alone, with your dog living on bones, and you, on hope—kindling each morning, dying slowly each night,—this could be borne. Philosophy would bring home its stores to the lone-man. Money is not in his hand, but Knowledge is in his brain! and from that brain he draws out faster, as he draws slower from his pocket. He remembers: and on remembrance he can live for days, and weeks. The garret, if a garret covers him, is rich in fancies. The rain if it pelts, pelts only him used to rain-peltings. And his dog crouches not in dread, but in companionship. His crust he divides with him, and laughs. He crowns himself with glorious memories of Cervantes, though he begs: if he nights it under the stars, he dreams heaven-sent dreams of the prisoned, and homeless Galileo.

He hums old sonnets, and snatches of poor Jonson's plays. He chants Dryden's odes, and dwells on Otway's rhyme. He reasons with Bolingbroke or Diogenes, as the humor takes him; and laughs at the world: for the world, thank Heaven, has left him alone!

Keep your money, old misers, and your palaces, old princes,—the world is mine!

> I care not, Fortune, what you me deny.—
> You cannot rob me of free nature's grace,
>   You cannot shut the windows of the sky;
> You cannot bar my constant feet to trace
>   The woods and lawns, by living streams, at eve,
> Let health, my nerves and finer fibres brace,
>   And I, their toys, to the great children, leave,
> Of Fancy, Reason, Virtue, naught can me bereave!

But—if not alone?

If *she* is clinging to you for support, for consolation, for home, for life—she, reared in luxury perhaps, is faint for bread?

Then, the iron enters the soul; then the nights darken under any sky light. Then the days grow long, even in the solstice of winter.

She may not complain; what then?

Will your heart grow strong, if the strength of her love can dam up the fountains of tears, and the tied tongue not tell of bereavement? Will it solace you to find her parting the poor treasure of food you have stolen for her, with begging, foodless children?

But this ill, strong hands, and Heaven's help, will put down. Wealth again; Flowers again; Patrimonial acres again; Brightness again. But your little Bessy, your favorite child is pining.

Would to God! you say in agony, that wealth could bring fulness again into that blanched cheek, or round those little thin lips once more; but it cannot. Thinner and thinner they grow; plaintive and more plaintive her sweet voice.

"Dear Bessy"—and your tones tremble; you feel that she is on the edge of the grave? Can you pluck her back? Can endearments stay her? Business is heavy, away from the loved child; home, you go, to fondle while yet time is left—but *this* time you are too late. She is gone. She cannot hear you: she cannot thank you for the violets you put within her stiff white hand.

And then—the grassy mound—the cold shadow of head-stone!

The wind, growing with the night, is rattling at the window panes, and whistles dismally. I wipe a tear, and in the interval of my Reverie, thank God, that I am no such mourner.

But gaiety, snail-footed, creeps back to the household. All is bright again;—

——the violet bed's not sweeter
Than the delicious breath marriage sends forth.

Her lip is rich and full; her cheek delicate as a flower. Her frailty doubles your love.

And the little one she clasps—frail too—too frail: the boy you had set your hopes and heart on. You have watched him growing, ever prettier, ever winning more and more upon your soul. The love you bore to him when he first lisped names—your name and hers—has doubled in strength now that he asks innocently to be taught of this, or that, and promises you by that quick curiosity that flashes in his eye, a mind full of intelligence.

And some hair-breadth escape by sea, or flood, that he perhaps may have had—which unstrung your soul to such tears, as you pray God may be spared you again—has endeared the little fellow to your heart, a thousand fold.

And, now with his pale sister in the grave, all *that* love has come away from the mound, where worms feast, and centers on the boy.

How you watch the storms lest they harm him! How often you steal to his bed late at night, and lay your hand lightly upon the brow, where the curls cluster thick, rising and falling with the throbbing temples, and watch, for minutes together, the little lips half parted, and listen—your ear close to them—if the breathing be regular and sweet!

But the day comes—the night rather—when you can catch no breathing.

Aye, put your hair away,—compose yourself—listen again.

No, there is nothing!

Put your hand now to his brow—damp indeed—but not with healthful night-sleep; it is not your hand, no, do not deceive yourself—it is your loved boy's forehead that is so cold; and your loved boy will never speak to you again—never play again—he is dead!

Oh, the tears—the tears; what blessed things are tears! Never fear now to let them fall on his forehead, or his lip, lest you waken him!—Clasp him—clasp him harder—you cannot hurt, you cannot waken him! Lay him down, gently or not, it is the same; he is stiff; he is stark and cold.

But courage is elastic; it is our pride. It recovers itself easier, thought I, than these embers will get into blaze again.

But courage, and patience, and faith, and hope have their limit. Blessed be the man who escapes such trial as will determine limit!

To a lone man it comes not near; for how can trial take hold where there is nothing by which to try?

A funeral? You reason with philosophy. A grave yard? You read Hervey and muse upon the wall. A friend dies? You sigh, you pat your dog,—it is over. Losses? You retrench—you light your pipe—it is forgotten. Calumny? You laugh—you sleep.

But with that childless wife clinging to you in love and sorrow—what then?

Can you take down Seneca now, and coolly blow the dust from the leaf-tops? Can you crimp your lip with Voltaire? Can you smoke idly, your feet dangling with the ivies, your thoughts all waving fancies upon a church-yard wall—a wall that borders the grave of your boy?

Can you amuse yourself by turning stinging Martial into rhyme? Can you pat your dog, and seeing him wakeful and kind, say, "it is enough?" Can you sneer at calumny, and sit by your fire dozing?

Blessed, thought I again, is the man who escapes such trial as will measure the limit of patience and the limit of courage!

But the trial comes:—colder and colder were growing the embers.

That wife, over whom your love broods, is fading. Not beauty fading;—that, now that your heart is wrapped in her being, would be nothing.

She sees with quick eye your dawning apprehension, and she tries hard to make that step of hers elastic.

Your trials and your loves together have centered your affections. They are not now as when you were a lone man, wide spread and superficial. They have caught from domestic attachments a finer tone and touch. They cannot shoot out tendrils into barren world-soil and suck up thence strengthening nutriment. They have grown under the forcing-glass of home-roof, they will not now bear exposure.

You do not now look men in the face as if a heart-bond was linking you—as if a community of feeling lay between. There is a heart-bond that absorbs all others; there is a community that monopolizes your feeling. When the heart lay wide open, before it had grown upon, and closed around particular objects, it could take strength and cheer, from a hundred connections that now seem colder than ice.

And now those particular objects—alas for you!—are failing.

What anxiety pursues you! How you struggle to fancy—there is no danger; how she struggles to persuade you—there is no danger!

How it grates now on your ear—the toil and turmoil of the city! It was music when you were alone; it was pleasant even, when from the din you were elaborating comforts for the cherished objects;—when you had such sweet escape as evening drew on.

Now it maddens you to see the world careless while you are steeped in care. They hustle you in the street; they smile at you across the table; they bow carelessly over the way; they do not know what canker is at your heart.

The undertaker comes with his bill for the dead boy's funeral. He knows your grief; he is respectful. You bless him in your soul. You wish the laughing streetgoers were all undertakers.

Your eye follows the physician as he leaves your house: is he wise, you ask yourself; is he prudent? is he the best? Did he never fail—is he never forgetful?

And now the hand that touches yours, is it no thinner—no whiter than yesterday? Sunny days come when she revives; color comes back; she breathes freer; she picks flowers; she meets you with a smile: hope lives again.

But the next day of storm she is fallen. She cannot talk even; she presses your hand.

You hurry away from business before your time. What matter for clients—who is to reap the rewards? What matter for fame—whose eye will it brighten? What matter for riches—whose is the inheritance?

You find her propped with pillows; she is looking over a little picture-book bethumbed by the dear boy she has lost. She hides it in her chair; she has pity on you.

——Another day of revival, when the spring sun shines, and flowers open out of doors; she leans on your arm, and strolls into the garden where the first birds are singing. Listen to them with her;—what memories are in bird-songs! You need not shudder at her tears—they are tears of Thanksgiving. Press the hand that lies light upon your arm, and you, too, thank God, while yet you may!

You are early home—mid-afternoon. Your step is not light; it is heavy, terrible.
They have sent for you.
She is lying down; her eyes half closed; her breathing long and interrupted.
She hears you; her eye opens; you put your hand in hers; yours trembles:—hers does not. Her lips move; it is your name.
"Be strong," she says, "God will help you!"
She presses harder your hand:—"Adieu!"
A long breath—another;—you are alone again. No tears now; poor man! You cannot find them!

——Again home early. There is a smell of varnish in your house. A coffin is there; they have clothed the body in decent grave clothes, and the undertaker is screwing down the lid, slipping round on tip-toe. Does he fear to waken her?

He asks you a simple question about the inscription upon the plate, rubbing it with his coat cuff. You look him straight in the eye; you motion to the door; you dare not speak.

He takes up his hat and glides out stealthful as a cat.

The man has done his work well for all. It is a nice coffin—a very nice coffin! Pass your hand over it—how smooth!

Some sprigs of mignionette are lying carelessly in a little gilt-edged saucer. She loved mignionette.

It is a good staunch table the coffin rests on:—it is your table; you are a house-keeper—a man of family!

Aye, of family!—keep down outcry, or the nurse will be in. Look over at the pinched features; is this all that is left of her? And where is your heart now? No, don't thrust your nails into your hands, nor mangle your lip, nor grate your teeth together. If you could only weep!

——Another day. The coffin is gone out. The stupid mourners have wept— what idle tears! She, with your crushed heart, has gone out!

Will you have pleasant evenings at your home now?

Go into your parlor that your prim housekeeper has made comfortable with clean hearth and blaze of sticks.

Sit down in your chair; there is another velvet-cushioned one, over against yours—empty. You press your fingers on your eye-balls, as if you would press out something that hurt the brain; but you cannot. Your head leans upon your hand; your eye rests upon the flashing blaze.

Ashes always come after blaze.

Go now into the room where she was sick—softly, lest the prim housekeeper come after.

They have put new dimity upon her chair; they have hung new curtains over the bed. They have removed from the stand its phials, and silver bell; they have put a little vase of flowers in their place; the perfume will not offend the sick sense now. They have half opened the window, that the room so long closed may have air. It will not be too cold.

She is not there.

——Oh, God!—thou who dost temper the wind to the shorn lamb—be kind!

The embers were dark; I stirred them; there was no sign of life. My dog was asleep. The clock in my tenant's chamber had struck one.

I dashed a tear or two from my eyes;—how they came there I know not. I half ejaculated a prayer of thanks, that such desolation had not yet come nigh me; and a prayer of hope—that it might never come.

In a half hour more, I was sleeping soundly. My reverie was ended.

—1850

Lucy Larcom 1824–1893

A writer by profession, Lucy Larcom supported herself as a poet and editor throughout most of her life—a rare feat for women at that time. While Larcom had the support of the activist poet John Greenleaf Whittier, a mentor and long-time friend, she became an accomplished writer in her own right. Born in Beverly, Massachusetts in 1824, Larcom spent much of her youth in the industrial community of Lowell, Massachusetts. Beginning at age eleven, she worked for over ten years in its cotton mills. Disliking the working conditions in the mill, Larcom ventured West to Illinois and what was then considered the frontier with her sister Emmeline in 1846. Larcom eventually accepted a job teaching at Monticello Academy in Alton, Illinois, where she also received a formal education for the first time. Larcom began writing poetry while working in the Lowell mills. A turning point in her career came in 1852, when she found her work included in the volume *Female Poets of America* by Rufus W. Griswold. In 1855, Larcom returned to teaching at Wheaton Academy in Norton, Massachusetts, although she grew increasingly discontented with the constraints the work placed on her writing time. During this time she published "A Loyal Woman's No" in *The Atlantic Monthly*, the most prominent literary magazine of the day. In 1864, Larcom left teaching in order to focus full time on her career as a writer. She published several poetry collections over the next twenty years, including *Poems* (1869) and *The Poetical Works of Lucy Larcom* (1884). In 1888, Henry O. Houghton approached Larcom and persuaded her to write her autobiography. *A New England Girlhood, Outlined from Memory,* was published in 1889 and related Larcom's girlhood experiences in the Lowell Experiment mills. This autobiography continues to offer a fascinating glimpse into its historical era. Always religious, Larcom turned to more devotional writings near the end of her life. Larcom died in 1893 in Boston.

Weaving

All day she stands before her loom;
    The flying shuttles come and go;
By grassy fields, and trees in bloom,
    She sees the winding river flow:
5 And fancy's shuttle flieth wide,
And faster than the waters glide.

Is she entangled in her dreams.
    Like that fair weaver of Shalott.[1]
Who left her mystic mirror's gleams,
10   To gaze on light Sir Lancelot?

[1] **Shalott:** Refers to "The Lady of Shalott," a poem by Alfred Lord Tennyson (1809–1892).

Her heart, a mirror sadly true,
Brings gloomier visions into view.

"I weave, and weave, the livelong day:
    The woof is strong, the warp is good:
15 I weave, to be my mother's stay;
    I weave, to win my daily food:
But ever as I weave," saith she,
"The world of women haunteth me.

"The river glides along, one thread
20   In nature's mesh, so beautiful!
The stars are woven in; the red
    Of sunrise; and the rain-cloud dull.
Each seems a separate wonder wrought;
Each blends with some more wondrous thought.

25 "So, at the loom of life, we weave
    Our separate shreds, that varying fall,
Some stained, some fair; and, passing, leave
    To God the gathering up of all,
In that full pattern, wherein man
30 Works blindly out the eternal plan.

"In his vast work, for good, or ill,
    The undone and the done he blends:
With whatsoever woof we fill,
    To our weak hands His might He lends,
35 And gives the threads beneath His eye
The texture of eternity.

"Wind on, by willow and by pine,
    Thou blue, untroubled Merrimack!
Afar, by sunnier streams than thine,
40   My sisters toil, with foreheads black;
And water with their blood this root,
Whereof we gather bounteous fruit.

"I think of women sad and poor;
    Women who walk in garments soiled:
45 Their shame, their sorrow, I endure;
    By their defect my hope is foiled:
The blot they bear is on my name;
Who sins, and I am not to blame?

"And how much of your wrong is mine,
50   Dark women slaving at the South?
Of your stolen grapes I quaff the wine;
    The bread you starve for fills my mouth:

The beam unwinds, but every thread
With blood of strangled souls is red.

55   "If this be so, we win and wear
          A Nessus-robe[2] of poisoned cloth;
      Or weave them shrouds they may not wear,—
          Fathers and brothers falling both
      On ghastly, death-sown fields, that lie
60   Beneath the tearless Southern sky.

      "Alas! the weft has lost its white.
          It grows a hideous tapestry,
      That pictures war's abhorrent sight:
          Unroll not, web of destiny!
65   Be the dark volume left unread,
      The tale untold, the curse unsaid!"

      So up and down before her loom
          She paces on, and to and fro,
      Till sunset fills the dusty room,
70   And makes the water redly glow,
      As if the Merrimack's calm flood
      Were changed into a stream of blood.

      Too soon fulfilled, and all too true
          The words she murmured as she wrought:
75   But, weary weaver, not to you
          Alone was war's stern message brought:
      "Woman!" it knelled from heart to heart,
      "Thy sister's keeper know thou art!"

—1884

Adah Isaacs Menken 1835?–1868

An actress, poet, and celebrity, Adah Isaacs Menken gained notoriety as a scandalous nineteenth-century stage personality. Menken married four men in the space of seven years at the height of her career and may have had as many as six husbands throughout her life. Her most famous stage performance was in H. M. Milner's Byronic play *Mazeppa,* where she played the role of a man and rode horseback wearing only flesh-colored tights, which caused her to appear nude. Many details about Menken's past remain unverifiable, largely due to Menken's own tendency to purposely obscure her

[2] **Nessus-robe:** Sometimes referred to as a shirt, in Greek mythology this item was given to Hercules by his wife and it poisoned him.

origins. She is believed to have been born in New Orleans in 1835 to Auguste Théodore, a free black, and Magdaleine Jean Louis Janneaux. She married her first husband, Alexander Isaac Menken, in 1856, and converted to Judaism—a religion she would assert as her own throughout her life. Menken rose to renown in 1861, thanks largely to the popularity of *Mazeppa*. Romantically linked to many famous men, such as the elder Dumas and the sexually ambiguous poet Swinburne, throughout her career, Menken's popularity came in part through a rumored preference for wild parties and sordid liaisons. While she is best known for her racy stage performances and transgressive offstage behavior, Menken also had a passion for poetry, often identifying herself as a poet. A volume of poetry published after her death, *Infelicia* (1869), contains the poem, "Judith," which serves as a complex exploration of gender and sexuality from a female perspective. Menken died in 1868 and was largely forgotten until 1938, when scholars renewed their interest in her life. Today, Menken presents a fascinating study in the mutability of race, gender, and sexuality—which occurs in her poetry, her performances, and her public reception.

Judith[1]

"Repent, or I will come unto thee quickly, and will fight thee with the sword of my mouth."—REVELATION ii. 16.

I.

Ashkelon. is not cut off with the remnant of a valley.
Baldness dwells not upon Gaza.
The field of the valley is mine, and it is clothed in verdure.
The steepness of Baal-perazim is mine;
And the Philistines spread themselves in the valley of Rephaim.[2]
They shall yet be delivered into my hands.
For the God of Battles has gone before me!
The sword of the mouth shall smite them to dust.
I have slept in the darkness—
But the seventh angel woke me, and giving me a sword of flame, points to the blood-ribbed cloud, that lifts his reeking head above the mountain.
    Thus am I the prophet.

---

[1] **Judith:** According to Jewish legend, Judith saved Israel by seducing and then beheading Holofernes, an enemy general.
[2] **Ashkelon … Rephaim:** Names of places located in the region of Palestine.

I see the dawn that heralds to my waiting soul the advent of power.

    Power that will unseal the thunders!

    Power that will give voice to graves!

    Graves of the living;

    Graves of the dying;

    Graves of the sinning;

    Graves of the loving;

    Graves of despairing;

And oh! Graves of the deserted!

These shall speak, each as their voices shall be loosed.

And the day is dawning.

II.

Stand back, ye Philistines!

Practice what ye preach to me;

I heed ye not, for I know ye all.

Ye are living burning lies, and profanation to the garments which with stately steps ye sweep our marble palaces.

Your palaces of Sin, around which the damning evidence of guilt hangs like a reeking vapor.

Stand back!

I would pass up the golden road of the world.

A place in the ranks awaits me.

I know that ye are hedged on the borders of my path.

Lie and tremble, for ye well know that I hold with iron grasp the battle axe.

Creep back to your dark tents in the valley.

Slouch back to your haunts of crime.

Ye do not know me, neither do ye see me.

But the sword of the mouth is unsealed, and ye coil yourselves in slime and bitterness at my feet.

I mix your jeweled heads, and your gleaming eyes, and your hissing tongues with the dust.

My garments shall bear no mark of ye.

When I shall return this sword to the angel, your foul blood will not stain its edge.

It will glimmer with the light of truth, and the strong arm shall rest.

III.

Stand back!

I am no Magdalene waiting to kiss the hem of your garment.

It is mid-day.

See ye not what is written on my forehead?

I am Judith!

I wait for the head of my Holofernes!

Ere the last tremble of the conscious death-agony shall have shuddered, I will show it to ye with the long black hair clinging to the glazed eyes, and the great mouth opened in search of voice, and the strong throat all hot and reeking with blood, that will thrill me with wild unspeakable joy as it courses down my bare body and dabbles my cold feet!

My sensuous soul will quake with the burden of so much bliss.

Oh, what wild passionate kisses will I draw up from that bleeding mouth!

I will strangle this pallid throat of mine on the sweet blood!

I will revel in my passion.

At midnight I will feast on it in the darkness.

For it was that which thrilled its crimson tides of reckless passion through the blue veins of my life, and made them leap up in the wild sweetness of Love and agony of Revenge!

I am starving for this feast.

Oh forget not that I am Judith!

And I know where sleeps Holofernes.

—1868